T.H. Hendley

London indo colonial exhibition of 1886

T.H. Hendley

London indo colonial exhibition of 1886

ISBN/EAN: 9783337764036

Printed in Europe, USA, Canada, Australia, Japan

Cover: Foto ©ninafisch / pixelio.de

More available books at **www.hansebooks.com**

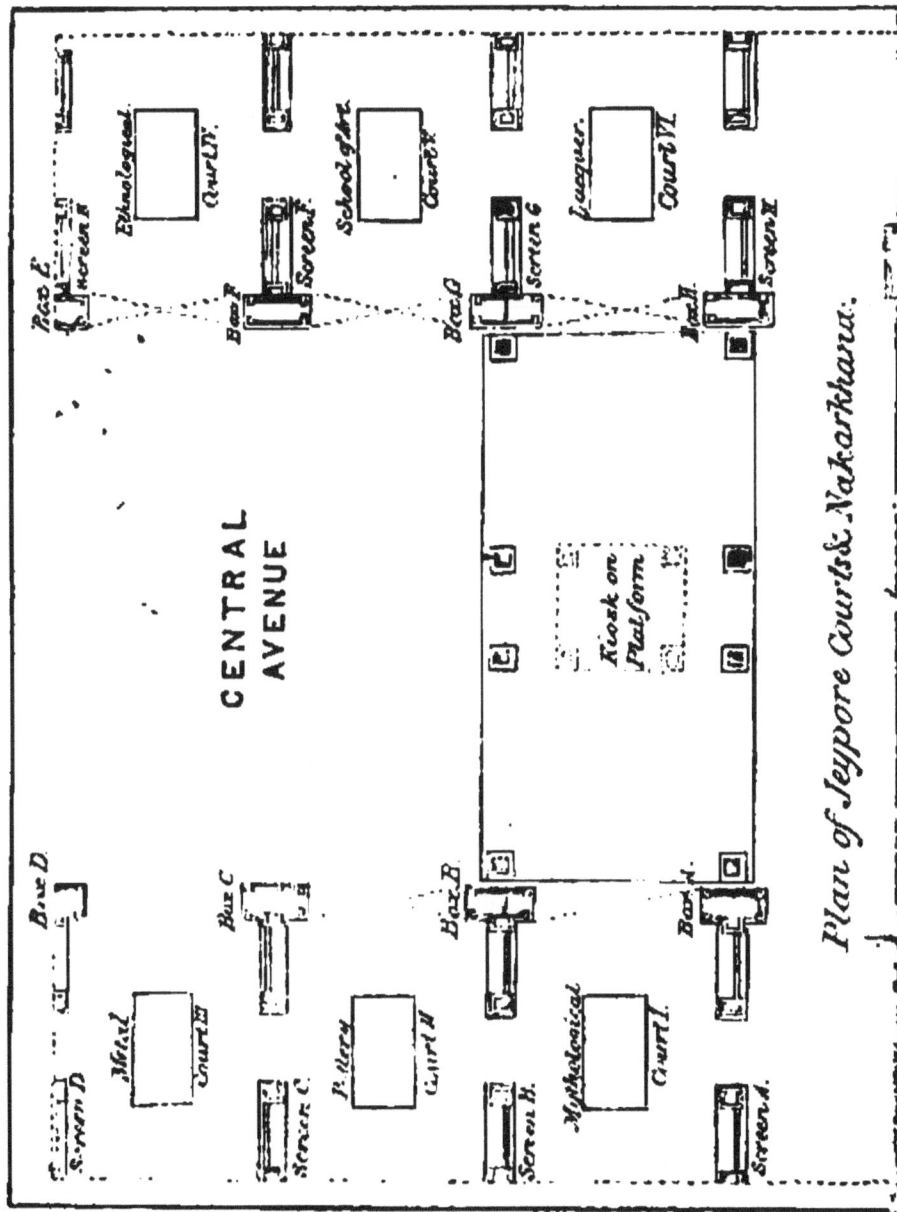

Plan of Jeypore Courts & Nakarkhana.

LONDON

JNDO-COLONIAL EXHIBITION

OF 1886.

HANDBOOK

OF THE

JEYPORE COURTS.

BY

T. H. HENDLEY, *Surgeon Major*, M.R.A.S. *and* M.A.S.B.,

HONORARY EXHIBITION OFFICER, JEYPORE.

CALCUTTA:

PRINTED BY THE CALCUTTA CENTRAL PRESS CO., LD.,

5, COUNCIL HOUSE STREET,

1886

CONTENTS.

iv CONTENTS.

CHAPTER I.

GENERAL DESCRIPTION OF JEYPORE.

JEYPORE, one of the largest and most important Rajput States, covers an area of 14,527 square miles, and lies between North Latitude 25° 43' and 28° 30', and East Longitude 74° 50' and 77° 18'. On the north it is bounded by Bikanir and the Punjab; on the east by Ulwar, Bhartpore and Karauli; on the south by Gwalior, Bundi, Tonk, Oodeyporo and Ajmero; and on the west by Kisheogarb, Marwar and Bikanir.

The general character of the country is level and open, but there are numerous ranges of hills and isolated peaks and ridges which diversify the scenery; and, as many of them are crowned with forts, and towns and villages are grouped round their bases, or stretch up the ravines on their sides, the beauty and picturesqueness of the country are much increased.

The centre of the State is an elevated tableland, at Jeypore 1,400 feet above the sea level. It rises towards the west and south and rapidly falls towards the east. On the Karauli border, and between the Chambal and Banas rivers, the country is very wild, and the scenery often beautiful. The Banas and Banganga rivers flow through the State. There are several smaller streams in Shekhawati, the northero province, some of which lose themselves in the sands; and there is one well known lake at Sambhar on the Jodhporo border, whence is produced an excellent kind of salt which is distributed through Northern India by the Imperial Inland Revenue Department.

The lake is leased to the Government of India, by the two States, which jointly own it; and its product is chiefly carried away by the Rajputana Railway, which, in a great measure, owes its origin to this salt deposit. The greater part of Jeypore belongs to what has been termed, from the principal feature io it, the Aravali geological region.

The rocks, which underlie the sand, and those which crop out above it, belong to the crystalline and transition series, in which to the present day no fossils have been discovered, and consequently their age has not been determined.

The Vindhyan rocks, from which the red sandstone of the Agra and Delhi forts was taken, touch them in the Hindown district, and are posterior to them in age. The Vindhian system is supposed to be older than the old red sandstone of Great Britain or than the Laurentian rocks.

The soil is made op of the *debris* of these rocks, and towards the east of alluvium or earth deposited from water and of sand blown op, it is thought, from the western seas.

In many places the earth is covered with a saline efflorescence known as "reh," which is injurious to cultivation. On the *red* soil the phenomenon of the mirage is often seen.

There are numerous salt sources in the State besides the Sambhar lake.

Kankar, a concretionary carbonate of lime of which Indian roads are so often made, is another product found in abundance in Jeypore. The lime in the *kankar* is of great value in agriculture, especially in the cultivation of cotton.

Many valuable building stones are quarried in the Jeypore territory. Examples of them in the rough and carved stato will be found in the Jeypore collection.

A little sandstone comes from Hindown near the Bhurtpore and Karaoli border.

Valuable marbles are obtained from the quarries of Bussi and Raialo in the north-east. Enormous slabs of mica schist, up to 30 feet in length, from the hill of Bankri close to the town of Dausa, are used throughout Jeypore for roofing purposes. The steatite, from which the Agra toys are made, is also, Mr. Hacket says, obtained from the Hindown district of Jeypore. Although the state is not rich in mineral wealth, copper, cobalt, and iron, especially the first two, have been obtained in paying quantities near Khetri. The scarcity of fuel is the chief difficulty in working the ores.

Garnets of the best kind, the finest in the world, it is believed, are found in the Rajmahal hills near the Banas, and beryl is also obtained.

The soil is generally sandy, and where there is but a scanty rainfall, as in Shekhawati, the crops are poor, and the population in consequence sparse, but on the sides of the water-courses and rivers, and in the beds of artificial tanks in more favoored regions, this apparently useless sand yields magnificent harvests.

In some places an abondant supply of grass is produced, upon which are reared the flocks of sheep that supply the Agra and Delhi districts with mutton.

From the physical aspect of the country to the history and social condition of its inhabitants is an easy transition.

CHAPTER II.

HISTORY.

THE early history of this part of India is very obscure, and the little that is known comes through sources from which much that is absurd and exaggerated must be eliminated.

The Meeoas of Jeypore may be ranked amongst the aboriginal races, which were driven into the mountains or deserts by wave after wave of hardy warriors, who entered India by its northern gates.

The first of the conquering hosts were, it is thought, Turanians, and are probably represented by the Dravidians of South India, the Jhâts of Bhartpore, and the Hindus of Shudra or low castes. After these came the Aryan ancestors of the Hindus of high caste.

It is impossible to say whether the Rajput is merely a division of the first Aryan invading tribe or a distinct offshoot from the grand old parent Central Asian stock from which the advanced races of both Europe and India have sprung.

The first historical event we have knowledge of is the great war between the Kauravas and Pandavas, the descendants of a king of Indraprastha or Delhi.

For twelve years the five famous Pandava brothers wandered, according to tradition, about Rajputana, and, during the thirteenth, they remained concealed in Bairot, to the north of Jeypore.

This family appears to have been one of many Rajput clans who established themselves in Northern India. At Nagar in the south of Jeypore, near Sambhar, and at Bairat, have been found traces of the residence of Buddhists, and of these the most famous is one of Asoka's inscriptions, dated about 250 B.C.

Chatsu, a town 25 miles south of modern Jeypore, belonged, it has been fairly well decided, to a contemporary or immediate ancestor of Vikramaditya, whose era is most commonly used in Rajputana to the present day. We are thus taken back to B.C. 56-57, the first year of the Sumvat era as it is called.[*]

Until the raid of Mahmud of Ghuzni in the year 1024, when he traversed Western Rajputana to reach the famous temple of Som-, nath, little further is known of the history of the land.

The country appears after this to have been ruled by a number of petty chiefs, one of whom was succeeded at Kho or Dausa by the first Rajah of Jeypore, about 1128 A.D. The history of the present ruling family must now, therefore, engage our attention.

His Highness the Maharajah of Jeypore is said to be the one hundred and thirty-ninth descendant in direct line from Kusa, the second son of Rama Chandra, the deified King of Oude, the hero of the Ramayana, one of the two great epic poems of India, by Sita an incarnation of Luchhmi, goddess of fortune, who was born from a furrow in the earth. Rama Chandra himself was reputed to be an avatar or incarnation of her husband Vishnu, the second member of the Trimurti or Hindu Trinity. The King was also sprung from the Sun, hence his descendants are known as the Surya-vansi or Suraj-bansi : the Children of the Sun. The early history of the family is obscure, but it was settled, it is believed, at a remote period at Rohtas on the Soane river, and then at Narwar and Gwalior, where, under the family designation of Pal, it ruled the neighbour-hood of those famous places until the reign of Tej Karan, who in the year A.D. 1128 left Gwalior for Deosa to marry Marool † the daughter of Raja Rao Mal, leaving his capital in the hands of a nephew who usurped the authority.

Tej Katao was therefore obliged to content himself with succeed-ing his father-in-law, whose town of Deosa or Dausa is close to the Rajputana Railway, about 35 miles east of Jeypore.

Tej Karan is generally known as Dulha Rai, the bridegroom king, who lost his throne for love of Macmi.

The local version of the story of his life is that his mother was driven from Narwar or Gwalior with her child, and that she took refuge with the Meena Chief of Khogaon in the hills, a few miles from Jeypore.

The infant's future fame was made known to her, in a not uncommon way, by a friendly cobra, who reared his head over the child as he slept.

The boy, when he became a man, repaid his Meena benefactor by slaying him, with his principal followers at a feast, which was held near a deep well still pointed out at Kho, and there founded his kingdom in blood. He then, according to this version, married Maroni and rendered himself famous by his love for her. The whole of modern Jeypore, as previously hinted, was ruled at that time by petty Rajput princes, some of the Chohan, others of the Bargujar clan, or by chiefs of the Meena tribe, a sturdy race which still forms the bulk of the population of the State. The early history of the Kachhwaha family, as it is called, was a constant struggle to increase their dominions, and thus Ramgarh was acquired, Amber, a Meena town to which the capital was removed, was taken, and many broad bigahs, or Indian acres, were added to the lands to which Dulha Rai had succeeded.

The fifth chief, Pajun, married the sister of Prithi Raj, the last Hindu King of Delhi and Ajmere, and fell with him on the fatal field of Narana A.D. 1193 in the struggle which gave India to Shahab-u-din Ghori.[*] Shaikhji, great grandson of Udekaran, the twelfth chief, was the ancestor of the Shekhawats[†] whose descendants occupy nearly the whole of the northern portion of the State, and now furnish some of the best recruits for our Indian army; while in days gone by, they supplied the Dakaits, or highway robbers, whose raids kept Central India in terror, only relieved by our successful efforts in rooting out the evil at its source. The Uniara Rajah, a Jeypore noble, and the Maharajah of Ulwar, are also descended from a younger son of Udekaran.

The seventeenth prince, Prithi Raj, left twelve sons, who attained their majority and became the ancestors of the twelve great families of Jeypore. After his death the Jeypore annals are fairly well

[*] Chand Bardai, the bard of Prithi Raj, and others, however, state that Pajun or Prajono was killed when fighting with Jai Chand, Rajah of Kanouj, shortly before.

[†] The Rajahs of Seekur and Khetri are Shekhawats.

known, as the vague and exaggerated Hindu accounts are confirmed by the works of the Mahomedan historians. Bahar Mal lived in the time of Humayun, Emperor of Delhi. His son, Bhugwantdas,[*] was a firm friend of Akbar, and from this friendship, which was continued by their sons and successors, and from the great talents of several of its princes, arose the superior position to which Jeypore has attained amongst the Rajpot States.

Man Singh, who succeeded Bhagwantdas about A. D. 1589, held the *munsab* or command of 7,000, under the emperor, who thus raised a Hindu above all the Mahomedan Officers of the Crown, and conquered Orissa for him.

He also made Assam tributary and was at different periods Viceroy of Bengal, Behar, the Deccan and Kabul.

He was the most prominent man of his time at the Imperial Court. In the Aln-i-Akbari, It is recorded that 60 of his 1,500 wives burned themselves on his funeral pile. The twenty-third prince, Jey Singh, known as the Mirza Rajah, held a command of 6,000 horse under the Moghuls, but, becoming too powerful for a subject, was assassinated by his own son at the instigation of the emperor. It is satisfactory to record that the parricide, and his descendants, were excluded for ever by the Rajpots from enjoying the throne which he coveted.

The twenty-seventh chief was the renowned Sawai Jey Singh, the famous astronomer, who founded the city of Jeypore, reformed the Indian Calendar, with the aid of observations made by him in the observatories, which he constructed at Jeypore, Delhi, Mathura, Benares, and Ujain; and was, besides being a liberal patron of art and science, a great politician and general.

The title "Sawai," which was given to him by the emperor of Delhi, and which his descendants have continued to hold, means one and a quarter, and was intended to indicate the very high estimation he was held in by his contemporaries. His brilliant labours will be noticed later on.

He made one great mistake, which led to ruin nearly overtaking both Jeypore and Oodeypore.

A treaty was agreed upon between these States and Jodhpore for common defence against the Mahomedan power, but unfortunately

---

[*] He saved the emperor's life near Sarnol. He was commander of 5,000 horse.

a coodition was made (to obtain the privilege of remarrying into the Oodeypore family which had been forfeited) that the sons of the queens of Oodeypore descent should succeed to the throocs of Jeypore and Jodhpore even in the event of there being elder boys by other wives.

Isri Singh, the eldest son of Jey Singh, succeeded his father, but Madho Singh, a much younger brother, the child of an Oodeypore princess, disputed the succession, and to ensure the victory the Maharaon of Oedeypore, his uncle, called in Holkar, the Mahratta, who overcame Isri Singh, who thereupon committed suicide.

Madho Singh succeeded and was a valiant prince, but the mischief was done, and from that time until the British supremacy in Rajputana was established to A.D. 1818, by treaties formed with all the native states in the Province, the whole country was overrun by the armies of Sindhia, Holkar, Meer Khan the first Nawab of Tonk, and others.

Under the three next chiefs, Prithi Siogh II, Partap Singh and Jagat Singh II, the country suffered greatly from these Incursions, and also from the loss of Macheri, a rich province, which in the time of Partap Singh secured its independence under one of the Jeypore nobles of the same name as the Rajah, who made it the nucleus of the important State of Ulwar.

A boy, Jey Singh III, was born a few months after the death of Jagat Singh, and the country was ruled in his name for 17½ years until his death In A.D. 1835, when Ram Singh succeeded and reigned until A.D. 1880. He not only maintained the reputation of his ancestors, but did immense good to his people, and secured so European reputation for his encouragement of art and learning, besides obtaining a conspicuous position for his loyalty and devotioo to the paramount British power. Maharajah Ram Siogh left no soos, but on his death-bed, he nominated, in accordance with Hindu law and custom, a young noble of his clan, a descendant of Jagat Singh I, to succeed him. This nomination was confirmed by the Government of India, and the new head of the Kachhwahas has assumed the name and style of Sawai Madho Singh, and has become the thirty-fifth Maharajah of Jeypore.

Since September 1882 he has enjoyed full powers of Government,* and, although he has only been five years on the throne, a large number of measures of great utility have been inaugurated, and all the institutions set on foot by his predecessors have been *kept up and flourish.*

* With certain restrictions which were removed in November 1883.

CHAPTER III.

—◇—

THE JEYPORE COURTS AND GATEWAY AT THE EXHIBITION.

THE gateway at the entrance of the Rajputana Court and the screens, which form the walls of the Jeypore bays, have been primarily constructed to afford more space for the display of exhibits, but they have been carved wherever possible to illustrate the position of wood-carving in the country. Jeypore, as a whole, is essentially a land of stone and stone-carvers, but, owing to the patronage of many wealthy bankers, who live in Shekhawati, the Northern District of the State, a large number of carpenters have settled in the great towns situated in that sandy tract, which is almost devoid of timber. Some of the better workmen, in past days, may, however, have been attracted from Delhi by the Musalman Nawabs of Futtehpore and Jhunjhunu, formerly rulers in the district. In the unsettled times, which preceded the British supremacy, the great capitalists of India, who were for the most part Marwaris of the branch of the Jain faith known as Oswals, sought safety, for which, of course, they well paid, among the chiefs and nobles who lived in Bikanir, Marwar, and Shekhawati, in other words on the verge of the country marked on our maps as the Great Indian Desert. In this way large towns have sprung up, such as Futtehpore, Nawalgarh, Jhunjhunu, Ramgarh and Chirawa, and here the bankers or Seths and their retainers have lived securely, while their agents or Gomasthas have earned in distant places, even as far as Hongkong on the one hand and Zanziber on the other, heavy interest on their capital. As the agents left their families at their homes, and retained little money, the heads of the firms ran but small risk.

The Seths have built magnificent temples and houses, and as good durable wood was scarce, they imported it from distant places, and had it carved into door frames, windows or balconies. Wonderful old traditional designs have thus been preserved.

Following this rule the writer suggested that the timber necessary for constructing the Jeypore Courts should be cut and joined in Bombay, and be then brought to Jeypore, where the Shekhawati carpenters should be allowed to enrich it by carving without unnecessary European interference. The scheme was adopted. The measurements of the screens were fixed in accordance with those laid down by the Royal Commission, and Colonel Jacob of Jeypore was good enough to put the ideas of the author into practical shape, by supplying a design for the screens, and an elevation for the entrance gate. In India the grand gateway of a temple or royal palace is usually surmounted by a chamber in which, at stated intervals, musicians play drums and other instruments in honour of the gods or of the sovereign. From the Arabic *nakara*, a *kettledrum*, the place has become known as the *Nakar-khana* or drum-house.

The Royal Commission accepted the Jeypore proposals to construct such an edifice at the entrance of the Rajputana Court. Theoretically it should have been a "Tripolia," or gate of three arches, but the necessities of the Exhibition have compelled its construction in its present form.

The general design is the modified Saracenic in vogue in Upper India and Rajputana. The only instructions issued to the woodcarvers have been that as great a variety of patterns was to be employed as possible ; the ornament was to be purely Indian, and no attempt was to be made to work on other than the traditional lines. The men drew rough outlines with a pencil or even the graver, and each carver has done what was right in his own eyes, subject to the approval of the *mistris* or master-workmen, who had to judge whether the whole work would be in harmony or not.

The screens were cut and joined by the Bombay Saw Mills Company, and the *Nakar-khana* by Mr. Wimbridge, Head of the East India Art Furnishing Company of Gawalia Tank Road, Bombay.

It has been urged that carving has been too lavishly employed, and that plain surfaces should have been left, by which the beauties of the ornamental work would have been the better displayed by contrast.

Apart from the fact that Indian, like mediæval European work, is characterised by the patient ornamentation of all parts that are unseen, as well as of those that are visible, there is the important consideration that, had our village carpenters been interfered with in their designs, it would have been impossible to tell where to stop, and the screens would have no longer been examples, as regards ornament, of pure Indian skill.

As it is now, the work is a good example of what uneducated men in the old time could accomplish. It must be recollected that all the carving will be within a few feet of the eye of the spectator in the position it will occupy in the exhibition, and that for this reason minuteness of detail has everywhere been justifiable. The endless variety of ornament, showing the fertility of invention, and the true artistic sense of the carvers, affords a field for much patient and pleasing study. Many of the workmen had never before left their homes in the desert. The general idea was that they were wanted in Kabul or even in distant England. Patience and the persuasive powers of Haji Mahomad Ali Khan, Nazim or Governor of Shekhawati, however, overcame the prejudices of a few men who came to Jeypore, and these soon induced others to follow their example.

They have worked cheerfully and well, and it has been most interesting to watch them as they laboured.

A little boy, whose photograph is sent to the exhibition, is a splendid carver. He has learned the art instinctively.

In his very earliest days he probably played by the side of his father as he carved, while his mother was engaged in some domestic occupation close by, or worked as a cooly near her husband. As soon as he could hold a piece of charcoal he would have begun to draw outlines on a board, sketching and re-sketching, it might be perhaps a flower or the features of Gunesh, the Elephant-headed God of Wisdom, who should be invoked at the beginning of all labour. In time, without conscious effort, and with a keen sense of pleasure, he could draw these objects with his eyes shut. Hand and eye insensibly acquired power and precision, so that his art became a part of his nature, at the time when his mind was most impressionable, and his fingers most capable of acting in unison with it. From drawing

he advanced to coarse carving of window or door frames er spin-
ning wheels, and, when entrusted with finer work, he copied the
designs of his father and his friends, and, perhaps, when he attains
manhood, be will one day hit upon a new design, which may be liked
by the craft and be imitated, and so become a permanent addition
to the number of grand traditional patterns which represent the
experience and sense of the beautiful of all ages and of all Oriental
wood-carvers since the world began, er it may be since the Babylo-
nians learned from the people of Accad the art, which they in turn
communicated to the Assyrians, and so on to the Persians, tho immediate art ancestors of his own craftsmen. It is the same with other
trades. The sculptor's son proceeds from drawing outlines en a
board to working in clay, and then to shaping in soap-stone rude
toys or images which are sold to the poor, and at last reaches the
royal marble, and produces those noble carvings which are the
astonishment and delight of visitors to the Kutb at Delhi, the Taj
at Agra, or tho great mosque at Ajmere. Another advantage gained
by this method is that, while children take in art like the food they
eat, their presence with their mothers at their fathers' work has a
purifying influence upon all. It is true the general standard of
refinement may not be high, but what there is, is the same for both
sexes and for all ages, and the society of children cannot but be
elevating, and tend to keep up a comparatively high degree of
innocence.

Our Shekhawati carpenters were no exception to this rule. They
were what one could imagine, the workmen who built the great
Cathedrals of Europe were—each man taking a part, not as a mere
machine, but as a creator bound down only to work on a certain
frame-work, and not to exceed certain limits, but with liberty to exert
the whole of his skill in building or decorating the special portion of
the structure allotted to him.

CHAPTER IV.

THE NAKAR-KHANA OR DRUM-HOUSE.

THE chamber over the gateway of royal residences or of temples is reserved for the accommodation of musicians who play at stated intervals, and in regular order, certain tunes in honour of the sovereign or god, after which other strains are added at the will of the performers.

The *Nakar-khana* which stands at the entrance of the Indian section of the Exhibition, has been constructed at the expense of the Maharajah of Jeypore, and was carved by his subjects in the way described in the previous chapter.

In the kiosk on the top are arranged all the musical instruments which are usually played in a drum-house. On the front of the platform has been carved the Shamsha or picture of the sun, which is symbolical of the descent of the lords of Jeypore and of the Rajput chiefs of the solar race, and is moreover according to the Ain-i-Akbari, or Institutes of the Emperor Akbar—"a Divine Light" which God directly transfers to Kings without the assistance of men. It is affixed to the gates or walls of palaces.

On the opposite side will be found a representation of the moon from which the Chandrabansi, the other great branch of the Rajput race, represented by the Rajahs of Jeysulmere and Karauli, is said to have sprung. On the same beam below the cornice on the front of the gate is engraved the motto of the Jeypore house " Yato dharm stato jaya"† in Sanskrit with Latin and English versions. The Latin " Ubi virtus ibi victor" better expresses the meaning of the original than the English " Where virtue is—is victory," but, however worded, the idea is as appropriate for the entrance of a great Exhibition as

---

* Also termed *Naubat-khana* from the larger drum used in it.

† Literally : " Where virtue or righteousness is – there is the victory.

it is for the motto of a State which has in many ways acted up to it. On the corresponding beam at the back the motto, "Ex Oriente lux," From the east comes light, has been carved.

The central kiosk can be closed with purdahs or curtains of mushru, that is cotton and silk cloth (silk alone was forbidden to be worn by Musalmans at prayer time, hence the fashion) of Indian make such as is used in Hindu palaces.

To support them chobs or metal poles have been provided.

The banners on the rails are respectively the *panch-rang* or five-coloured flag of Jeypore ; a small copy of the standard given to the late Maharajah at the Imperial Assemblage at Delhi by H. M. the Queen Empress ; the *Mahi maratib* or symbol of the highest nobility given by the Moghul Emperors, which was much prized.

It consists of the golden head of a fish and of two gilt balls, all borne on separate poles.

These symbols were brought from Delhi in the reign of the Emperor Feroksher, and so great was the honour deemed that the musicians in the Jeypore *Nakar-khana* played for three days and nights consecutively and the whole city was given up to rejoicing.

CHAPTER V.

RELIGION AND MYTHOLOGY.

MYTHOLOGY is the key to Hindu art, or at all events to the motive which is at the bottom of all decorative work done by the Hindu.

Jeypore supplies nearly all Brahmanical India with its stone images, and stone is the most orthodox material for use in temples.

For these two reasons, a small typical collection, in which most of the common mythological forms are represented, is appropriately displayed in the first Jeypore Court at the entrance of an Indian Exhibition. The images have been made on the same scale, a small one, in order that they may be the more easily studied, and great care has been taken in carving and painting the symbols by which they are distinguished. These are usually, though not always, contained in the hands, which are numerous where it is proposed to represent omnipotence.

In some cases a difference in colour is of prime importance. Moreover, most of the gods have a special vehicle or *vahan*, which is also adored in the hope that his vicarious influence may benefit the worshipper.

It is hardly necessary to observe that there are numerous sects of Brahmanical Hindus, besides several great schismatic faiths, the most prominent of which are the Jain and Sikh.

Of orthodox Hindus (the word is used here only in a religious sense) there are two great divisions—the followers of Vishnu and those of Siva or Mahadeo ; for practically Brahma is not worshipped in this age, and has only one temple in all India, that at Pushkar, near Ajmere.

Many branches of each sect exist who revere the deity in some particular incarnation, and although a Vaishnava or follower of Vishnu, for example, goes to temples of that deity most frequently, he does not altogether neglect Siva. The Hindu is very catholic in his ideas and is ready to adore any new manifestation of accredited powers. In this way a number of demi-gods are revered.

A description of all the ordinary images which have been exhibited will be found in the list of contents of the courts.

THE JAINS.

A large number of the most wealthy merchants and bankers in Rajputana follow the Jain faith.

It is everywhere spoken of as a most ancient religion, "*Bahot párána mat,*" and recent writers have asserted that it was a prominent faith at the beginning of our era, and was parallel with, if not the parent of, Buddhism.

By Brahmanical Hindus the Jains are looked upon as atheists (*nastic*), that is, those who believe in a future state, which is only attained by the result of their deeds (*karm*). They thus deny the power of the Almighty to influence their future.

Their duties are : (1) mercy to all animated beings ; (2) alms-giving ; (3) venerating the sages when living and worshipping their images when deceased ; (4) confession of faults ; and (5) religious fasting.

They should avoid the sins of (1) killing ; (2) lying ; (3) stealing ; (4) adultery ; and (5) worldly-mindedness.

There are two great divisions of their body—the Svetâmbaras [*] or those who worship images clothed and adorned with jewels, and the Digambaras[+] or those whose images are nude. There are, however, it is said, 84 points of distinction, one being that the latter division holds that women must undergo another birth (for they all believe in transmigration of souls), in other words, become men before they can attain *moksâ*, that is, salvation or beatitude.

They all revere twenty-four deified saints, lords, Tirthankaras or Jinas. These are all shewn on a lacquered panel and separately as stone images.

The following is a list, in order, of the Tirthankaras, with their symbols, which are placed on the pedestals and are the means of

---

[*] Those who clothed in white.
[+] Those whose clothing is the four cardinal points, *i.e.*, who are naked.

distinguishing them. The prevailing colour is yellow or golden, but there are exceptions to this rule.

Names.		*Symbols.*
1. Rishabha	...	... A bull.
2. Ajita	...	... An elephant.
3. Sambhava	...	... A horse.
4. Abhinandana	...	... An ape.
5. Sumati	...	... A curlew.
6. Padmaprabha	...	... A lotus.
7. Suparswa	...	... A swastica or ⌙ shaped sign.
8. Chandraprabha	...	... The moon.
9. Pushpadanta	...	... An alligator.
10. Sitala	...	... A srivatsa, or shaped curl.
11. Sreyan	...	... A rhinoceros.
12. Vasupujya	...	... A buffalo.
13. Vimala	...	... A boar.
14. Ananta	...	... A falcon.
15. Dharma	...	... A thunderbolt.
16. Santi	...	... An antelope.
17. Kunthie	...	... A goat.
18. Ara	...	... A nandyavarta.
19. Malli	...	... A jar.
20. Munsuvrata	...	... A tortoise.
21. Nimi	...	... A blue water lily.
22. Nemi	...	... A conch shell.
23. Parswanatha	...	... A hooded snake.
24. Mahavira	...	... A lion.

Numbers 6 and 12 have a red complexion; 8 and 9 are fair; 19 and 23 are blue or green; and 20 and 22 are black; the rest are yellow or golden. A series of lacquered boards used as covers for small Jain books or *pothis* is exhibited. Each has painted upon it a scene of interest connected with the faith. Some of the stories are very quaint, and not unlike those with which Europeans are familiar, such as one resembling that of Joseph and Potiphar's wife, or of the king who promised to redeem a bird, which a hunter had taken, with an equal weight of his own flesh, and who then found that the whole of his body was insufficient to turn the scale, and that the bird proved to be the god of righteousness himself, who of course rewarded him. A large shrine carved in brass is also exhibited. It is carved with Jain lucky emblems in relief, and as a whole represents the *samosaran* or throne prepared by Indra for the Tirthan-karas to sit upon when preaching their doctrines. Four images of Rishabha or Adinath the first Lord, to whom this particular shrine is supposed to be dedicated, have been placed on the top seat to indicate that the people below saw the pontiff's face from whichever side they happened to be. The Jains also believe that there are many com-partments in heaven and in hell. The former are usually represented as somewhat monotonous in character, while in the latter no com-plaint can be made of want of variety; for each inhabitant is being tormented by demons in a fashion appropriate to the sins he has committed in the world. Of course, cruelty to animals is most cruelly punished, but the lowest depth is reached by women who have told falsehoods to their husbands.

The Jains have always been wealthy, and they have ever devoted their gains to the honour of their religion. The well-known temples at Abu were built by Jains, and a magnificent fane at Sanganir, 7 miles south of Jeypore, about 900 years old, photographs of which are exhibited, attests the splendour of their gifts and the marvellous skill of the workmen and artists who carried out their ideas.

There is hardly anything in India more impressive or more richly and elaborately decorated than the grand Jain altar at Sanganir. A model in brass, gilt and adorned with floral ornament, is another illustration of their devotion to religion and of the mode in which much of the wealth of India is buried in unproductiveness in temples. It is a reproduction of a small portion of a grand model in brass and gold, which a rich banker is constructing to place in a temple he has built in Ajmere. It is understood that this model, which covers a large space and will cost a lakh of rupees, or £7,500, represents the city that Indra, the Vedic king of the Celestials, gave to Rikhabdeo or Rishabha at his birth, and that the generous donor hopes for no reward in this world, but humbly trusts that in the life to come he will secure accommodation on a similar scale, and be surrounded by as many attendants there as he has represented in his model here in the form of small metal figures. This is the popular idea, his own explanation is that he has been actuated by a desire to teach his poorer co-religionists. Most of the wealthy bankers, who patronize the wood carvers in Shekhawati, are Jains. Outside rupees and the arithmetical calculation connected with their accumulation, they seem to have no idea of figures ; for their deified saints are said to have lived for many ages and their geographical measurements are illimitable. Their idea of the world is not unlike that of the Hindus, as a map of the Jain universe sufficiently shows.

The seas of milk and curd surround seven worlds of different kinds, and within is the home of the blessed, a sort of garden of Eden, watered by four great streams which flow out from the abode of the celestials.

CHAPTER VI.

STONE CARVING AND DECORATIVE WORK.

As might be anticipated in a country abounding with stone, carving in that material is quite a speciality of Jeypore and the neighbouring districts. A little work is done in red sandstone, and chiefly in the east at Hindown and Sawai Madhopore, where rocks of that formation are at hand, but most of the good carving in Jeypore is executed in the more royal marble which is found in a number of places. The purest is obtained from Makrána on the borders of Marwar, west of the Sambhar lake, but is largely utilized in Jeypore in the manufacture of images, which are sent to all parts of India, and of which a selection is exhibited in the first court. They are plain, coloured, or gilt. At Dausa, east of the capital, large numbers of idols are made, for export towards Gujerat, from a veined whitish-blue marble from Raialo, in the hills near Ulwar.

A whole division of the city of Jeypore is devoted to the silawats or stone-cutters, who, besides their ordinary work, now find employment under the Executive Engineer, Col. Jacob, under whose guidance they have, during the past few years, turned out carvings which are much more highly finished than formerly. Figures are also carved in black and red marble, and decorative carving is executed in a cream-coloured stone which has been much admired in Europe. The quarries are situated at Bussi in the Jeypore State.

The nummulitic limestones of Jeysulmore are also cut at Jeypore into slabs for pavements ; and a soft chlorite from Dungarpora is worked into small images and toys. On these soft stones as well as on steatite the boys learn to carve.

When in Jeypore early in 1885, Mr. C. Purdon Clarke ordered a copy to be made in Makráns marble of a well known local design for a window. The work has been executed and is exhibited in the first court on the left of the entrance to the Indian section.

Two panels in the same marble have also been prepared. They are exact reproductions of originals from the plinth of the cenotaph of Maharajah Sawai Jey Singh, the founder of Jeypore.

The figures are beautifully carved, and it will be seen that the marble is capable of taking a high polish.

The images in the central case, in Court I, are also in white marble, and some larger specimens, shown in Court II, are of the same material, coloured and gilt in accordance with the usual rule. The Buldeogarh red or salmon-coloured marble has been shown in the form of camels and other animals, and there are a few specimens of a similar kind, and one large image, a Jain Lord, in black marble of Bainslana in Jeypore.

A full-sized copy of a pretty little wayside shrine in one of the main streets in the capital has been prepared as an illustration of a common use to which marble is put in Jeypore. The total cost of the stone and workmanship on the spot was one hundred and eighty-five rupees.

From work in stone the transition to plaster is natural. The Jeypore plaster or *araiish* is famous throughout Rajputana. Walls, floors and dadoes, covered with this beautifully cool-looking material, which takes a high polish, may be found in every house of importance in Jeypore.

The white smooth floors can be easily kept clean, and, amongst a people who do not use shoes within doors, long retain their brilliancy of surface.

The dados are usually enriched with floral or other patterns in black or the primary colours. Colonel Jacob of Jeypore has developed and extensively employed this art in decorating new buildings in the capital.

In one of the top panels of Court IV will be found a number of plaques showing how this work may be utilized. In some water, in others oil, has been the medium for the colours employed. Opposite to this series is another, in which the ornament is formed from pieces of glass backed with foil of different colours.

Plaster of Paris or *gach* is obtained from Nagore in Marwar, and after it has set a piece of the necessary size is taken, and a design traced upon it by means of stencil papers and ink.

The glass and foil are then applied with gum and plaster, and the whole again covered with a sheet of plaster alone.

The portions of glass that are intended to be seen are exposed by cutting away the plaster above them with fine tools. This work is termed *jamla gach ki jilli.*

The panels above the two central front screens have been filled up with plaques, in which the pattern is formed by pieces of glass of different colours set between two sheets of plaster in such a way that the light can be seen through the design, the whole having the appearance of a jewelled window. This work is known as *gach ki jilli.*

One of the panels in the metal Court has been filled with glass mosaic or *jarao,* in which the colours are fixed by heat, and Chandras or Canada Balsam, to the inner surface of pieces of glass, which are attached to a base of plaster or stone by gum. The lines of junction are gilded, and metal foil and mercury are applied to the back of each piece of glass. The upper part of the front screen of Court IV contains specimens of mirror work, such as is commonly employed in ornamenting the ceilings of bath-rooms, palaces, or *Shish Mahals.* In all these the design is formed by small convex pieces of silvered glass, or even mica, enriched by outlines in plaster covered with silver or gold, and by the occasional introduction of bright colours.

The top of the third front screen contains a number of brass vessels, each fitting into a niche cut purposely to receive it.

Travellers are often puzzled at seeing the sides of rooms covered with paintings of vessels of different shapes.

These represent all that is left of an old Persian custom by which niches were made in the walls of halls and rooms to receive the gold or silver vessels belonging to the house. In this way it became easy to ascertain when a vase was missing.

The vessels exhibited have been restored from the outlines on the walls of the Amber palaces.

The upper portions of two of the screens in the first and sixth Courts have been fitted with small tiles of Jeypore pottery set in frames. Each of these tiles when taken down can be used as a teapot or kettle stand.

A drawing in blue monochrome on Jeypore tiles has been placed in one of the niches in the screen between the first and second Courts on the left hand. It represents the Hawa Mahal or palace of the wind at Jeypore. In a similar niche on the opposite side of the screen a picture of the great gate of the palace at Amber has been fixed. This portal a noted authority considers the finest entrance to a large building in the world.

CHAPTER VII.

POTTERY.

A LARGE collection of semi-translucent pottery is shewn in the second and fifth Courts, and above the entrance archways of the latter as well as of the fourth Court.

It was not until the opening of the School of Art in 1866 that pottery of any value was made in Jeypore, but since that date a large quantity has been produced. Practically it is the same as that for which Delhi has been long noted. The yellow clay and felspar, which are the principal ingredients in its manufacture, are, however, obtained in the state, and the cobalt and copper, with which it is coloured, are also found near Bhagore on the property of the Rajah of Khetri, a feudatory of Jeypore. The vessels are formed in moulds, and, after union of the separate parts, are coated with powdered white felspar mixed with starch, and are then painted. The blue colour, which is most characteristic of the work, is obtained from an oxide of cobalt (a specimen of this ore, which is known under the name of Syepoorite or Jeypoorite, is exhibited), and the green from an oxide of copper, which is associated with it in the mines. The ware is then dipped in a transparent glaze of glass and when dry goes to the kiln. Only one baking is required.

The variety of the designs is immense ; in fact the great difficulty seems to be to reproduce any particular pattern. Most of the vases exhibited have been decorated with arabesque patterns. Of late the potters have preferred to cover their vessels with mythological and other figures, but, as the results are neither artistic nor pleasing, very few examples of this kind of work have been sent to London.

The tiles in the first and second Courts (see page 24) have been made in this ware at the School of Art.

In the fifth Court a few specimens of clay pottery, some of which have been painted, are shewn.

As every article is hand painted and the designs are so rarely repeated, the prices are necessarily somewhat higher than those charged by European potters, but the purchaser has the pleasure of knowing, when he becomes the possessor of a Jeypore vase, as is the case with so many other articles of Indian manufacture, that he owns something that has required an individual effort of mind to produce, something in short which is not a mere mechanical repetition of the design of another person.

CHAPTER VIII.

JEWELLERY AND PLATE.

Garnet Jewellery.

THE Jeypore garnets are in very great demand throughout India and in Europe, and in fact are so cheap and superior that they have practically driven the produce of other mines out of the market.

The trade is now carried on as a branch of the Jeypore Government Revenue Department under the management of Mr. S. J. Tellery.

The stones are found in the Jeypore, Oodeypore, and Kisheogarh States, but the best are now quarried in the first-named territory, at a place not far from Rajmahal on the Banas river, and close to the hills overlooking the estate of the Thakur of Duni. The quarries vary much in depth.

Garnets are often found on the surface, but most frequently as far down as sixty feet. The matrix in which the stones are imbedded is mica schist or serpentine, and the crystals are usually of dodecahedral form, as is clearly shown in two large examples in the collection.

Large gems are often found. A very clear stone cut en cabochon, which weighs 2·77 ounces, is exhibited. It is worth Rs. 150 in Jeypore.

For the European market most of the stones were formerly exported in the rough, but as a large number of workmen, chiefly boys, are being trained under a skilled European lapidary at Jeypore, many of the garnets are now cut on the spot.

The selected stones are generally polished into carbuncles or cabochons, which are known in the trade as tallow tops, as they are not unlike a drop of tallow, being convex above and concave or flat below.

This form best displays the peculiar fire and beauty of the gem.

Stones for rings and necklaces are cut into facets, and for the latter purpose are strung on silk by a special class of work-people in

Jeypore. A number of ornaments with gold setting is shewn. Gold, of course, is the best metal for this purpose, but enormous quantities of trinkets, in which the setting is of silver, are sold, for the gem is cheap and largely worn by the peasantry of many countries.

The colours vary from yellow with a brown tinge to purple; the latter are the most valuable, and are the real almandine or noble garnets.

Enamelling.[*]

It has been asserted that enamelling is the master art of the world, and for enamelling on gold Jeypore is acknowledged to be pre-eminent. Some work is also done ee silver and copper, and examples of all kinds are exhibited. For a full account of this art the writer must refer the reader to a paper of his own in Part II, Journal of Indian Art for 1884.

The Jeypore enamel is of the kind termed Champléve, the outline being formed by the plate itself, while the colours are placed in depressions hollowed out of the metal. These colours are metallic oxides, and are made to adhere by fire; they are applied in succession for each single tint or group of tints. It is this necessity of repeated exposure to varying temperatures, depending upon the different lengths of time required by the colours before they fuse, that makes the art of the enameller so difficult, and the risk run at every stage of course greatly increases the value of the ornament thus decorated. The red colour is the most difficult to apply, and for this hue Jeypore is famous. These facts must be taken into consideration when examining enamels. Like the minute bronzes of the Japanese the more this work is studied the greater appear its beauties. Gems are also used to enhance the richness of the enamel. As few artists are engaged in this work, the outturn is very limited. As the South Kensington Museum contains some large pieces, it has not been considered necessary to contribute many expensive articles oo the

---

[*] See also "Jeypore enamels, from designs furnished by Colonel Jacob," Jeypore, and "Memorials of the Jeypore Exhibition," by Surgeon-Major T. H. Hendley. Both published by W. Griggs, Peckham, and shewn in the Exhibition.

present occasion, but a considerable stock of jewellery, in which enamelling forms the principal feature, has been sent. The largest specimen shewn is a box especially prepared for the Royal Commission in which the ornament is of a simple character, and the colours are pure primary tints and few in number; for in enamel, as in so much modern Indian work, the tendency has been to excess of ornament, and a great multiplicity of hues, some of which are crude and wanting in harmony.

The kairi, or small locket in the form of an unripe mango, the fish-shaped charms, whistles, breastpins, rings and bracelets are sent in considerable numbers, as these articles are most appreciated by Europeans.

Enamel is much used in India as a foil to gems, especially in the decoration of arms, in which a maximum of effect is obtained by the use of diamond scales and flat stones with a minimum of expense.

It will be seen also that the quasi-enamel of Pertabgarh is often used for the backs of brooches, and the plaques of necklaces in contrast with the true enamel. The bracelets are hollow, and are filled with a composition which prevents them from injury.

The Jeypore enamel stands great climatic changes without chipping or scaling off, and in this respect is superior to much that is made in Europe.

The enamel is exhibited in the cases in Court II.

Gold and Silver Jewellery.

The forms of Indian jewellery are as endless as is the demand for it. In prosperous times all classes invest their savings in this manner, and no girl can become a bride without, for her position in life, a really considerable outlay on ornaments for her person, which serve as her dowry, and as a provision for her family in times of need. Sooner or later, however, her gold and silver are sure to be sold or find their way to the melting pot, and thus it is that the most ancient forms are found in the base metals ornaments which are worn by the poor, especially by the Brinjarras or wandering grain merchants, for the material of which they are made has no great intrinsic value. Moreover the farther from Delhi or the sea board the place of manufacture, the more Hindu, the more archaic, and usually the more massive are the ornaments.

The jewels of a head queen often weigh as much as forty pounds, while the burden of the lace of the hem of the many-folded skirt of her dress may come to as much more.

Gold jewellery is worn by all who can afford it; silver is the metal of the poorer classes, and there are certain castes or trades, such as the butchers, which, under native rule, were not permitted to use the more valuable metal. Many of these sumptuary or class laws or customs are, however, falling into abeyance.

A small selection of gold jewellery worn by the Jeypore people will be found in the central case in Court II.

One or two pieces are worthy of special attention, and the first is a string of large circular discs alternating with smaller ones and with beads.

This magnificent ornament, known under the name of "Haikal," is worn across the waist in such a way as to hang loosely over the opposite thigh.

A large neck jewel reminds one of the ancient collars of gold of Europe.

The massive gold anklets are such as are worn by persons of rank; in fact the privilege of wearing these, amongst men, is only accorded, in Hindu Courts, to nobles of the first class or "tazimis" and to princes.

In a necklace with bell-shaped drops, we recognize pendants of very old form; here we have exact reproductions of the Buddhist or Jain bell, such as is seen attached to a chain in the sculptures on pillars of a very early period. The barley-shaped drops of one of the bracelets and of a necklet show how the Hindu loves to imitate natural objects, or at least to take a hint from them.

The "Arya" or necklet with triangular pendants comes from Marwar, the Great Western Rajput State with which the Jeypore nobles have intimate relations by marriage. In type it is decidedly Assyrian.

There is also an ornament for the upper arm composed of small cylindrical cases in which written charms may be securely kept and worn.

An example of filagree jewellery is sent, but this style of work is more characteristic of Delhi and of Mahomedan centres.

A large number of silver ornaments, such as are in common use in Jeypore and throughout Rajputana, is displayed in the collection.

Amongst them are the same forms as are exhibited in silver, but there are many others of interest, such as the bracelets with bunches of grape-like drops, which are much worn by Hindu women ; a peculiar set of toe rings united by chains ; and an ornament for the froot of the foot, and a similar ornament for the hand and fingers known as "bath phul."

There are also bracelets, composed of shell-shaped pieces threaded on silk, others with bell-shaped pendants or tassels, and some of solid rings of metal, but, however solid the ornament may be, there is always some attempt at decoration. The pierced bracelet or "Neurl," though worn by women, is most often made on a large scale for state horses on whose legs it is fastened, when filled with small pieces of pebbles or metal, in order that a tinkling noise may be produced as the animal ambles along beneath its proud rider in a procession.

The enormous weight of the anklets will account for the elephant gait of the women, of which the Oriental poet loves to write, and the bells and minute pendants of both foot and arm-ornaments give rise to the tinkling harmony which accompanies the rapid movements of the Indian "Natch girl."

Very little alloy is used in making silver jewellery, and the cost of manufacture is trifling.

The more simple ornaments, which are used as investments of savings, are cast and fashioned from the rupees of the owner, as she sits beside the workmen, and are as easily melted up when required.

Plate.

Only a small quantity of silver plate is contributed, because the Hindu rarely uses any but perfectly plain vessels, which can be easily cleansed by much washing or rubbing with sand or earth. Such treatment would be fatal to engraved or chased work.

In the case of the Atrdan or perfume stand, such as the one exhibited, these considerations are not of moment as the piece does not require violent rubbing when it is necessary to clean it. So also with the beautifully pierced and chased pan or betel boxes, one of which is shaped like the betel leaf itself. The trays, which are shewn, are chiefly used for bearing the prepared pan and cardamoms when they are to be distributed to guests at the conclusion of a visit; some of these are parcel gilt in accordance with the fashion in Central India, and especially in the Mahomedan state of Tonk. The canopy in the interior of the Jain shrine is an example of a use to which silver is put.

Much of the wealth of the mercantile classes amongst the Hindus is lavished upon the images for their gods, and on the numerous articles used in religious worship, such as censors, lamps, spoons and bowls, whilst the rich nobles love to adorn their court furniture or vehicles and the trappings of their animals with the precious metals. Some of the best surface patterns are found on the clobs or maces carried by peons or chaprasies, or on the pillars which support curtains. Some of these of copper, plated with silver, have been sent. Four of these poles have been used to support the curtains of the Nakar-khana, and similar work will be found on the handles of the Chamaras, or plumes of yak tails, and of the morchals or peacock-feather fly whisks of state, which have been placed in one of the cases. In the School of Art Court is displayed a collection of engraved silver.

Here also is some work of a man trained at the Rurki School of Engineering, who has introduced into Jeypore and Ulwar a method of ornamenting burnished silver or gold surfaces with spirited figures of animals, or birds, or insects, in the midst of well drawn foliage. The natural fur and feathers are skilfully imitated; this, of course, is not a very appropriate treatment of the surface of a vessel intended for much use, but it is ingenious. Unfortunately the articles thus ornamented are too often European in form.

A Bokhara-shaped coffee-pot is a handsome piece of plate, but

as much cannot be said for a vase, with grotesque handles and
spout and busts on the bowl, which is an adaptation from the
drawing of a vessel in the hands of a demon king in the Emperor
Akbar's copy of the Razmnamah, a translation of the Mahabharata
or great Hindu epic.

A massive silver paper knife, with ornament taken from a dagger
in the Jeypore Armoury, and a collection of quasi-Apostle spoons,
with Hindu demigods on the handles in the room of the
Saints, will illustrate the facility with which the Indian workmen can assimilate European ideas, or be led by European guides.
A goblet with a pierced cover, which is exhibited by the State, is a
copy of one made for the use of a native princess.

The School of Art contributes a massive silver *hookah*, a very
appropriate use of the metal in India, where this article is the cyno-
sure of all beholders in the guest chamber of a native gentleman.
H. H. the Maharajah has also lent a very handsome old *hookah* of
parcel-gilt silver.

The figures of dancing girls and musicians, which adorn the bowl
and fire receptacle or *chillam*, are very spirited and well finished.
A dainty little mouthpiece for the *nechwa* or *hookah* pipe, made of
silver, parcel-gilt and jewelled, and shaped in the form of a female
figure, is worth examination.

A silver tray, sent by the School of Art, is a small imitation of
one which was made for presentation at the instance of the writer,
who acted upon a suggestion made some years before by Colonel
Jacob, that some of the ornamentation of the old tombs at Delhi
should be thus utilized. This subject will be fully treated in the
next chapter.

Attention cannot be drawn too often to the great drawback to the
sale of Indian plate in England caused by the unsatisfactory state
of the law on the subject, which compels all articles to be *Hall
marked*, under conditions, which Indian plate cannot, for technical
reasons, easily satisfy.

CHAPTER IX.

WORK IN BRASS AND OTHER BASE METALS.

As the vessels in common domestic use amongst the Hindus are nearly always made of brass, a large number of braziers (in Jeypore about a hundred families) finds ample employment in manufacturing them. A collection of the ordinary household utensils has been contributed. These include a few made of mixed metal and of copper.

Copper and tinned iron are principally used by Mahomedans. It has already been observed that the Hindu purifies his metal vessels by daily scouring with sand, hence there is very little attempt to enrich the surfaces by ornament of any kind. There is, however, a tendency to change in this direction, which has been met at Jeypore, in the School of Art, by the production of a good deal of engraved brass, especially of Ganges waterpots and vessels used in temples, which are covered with engraved mythological figures. Small soap and betel boxes are made in the school, and are sold in the open market. They are engraved and pierced with floral designs, some of them in panels, with chased figures of small birds and animals introduced into the midst of the foliage. A large oval tray shown in Court III, covered with chased and engraved figures, is the best example of this kind of brass work yet made in the School of Art.

In the section on silver plate reference was made to some brass trays, with borders worked in Arabesque designs in *repoussé*, which have been recently introduced. They are exact reproductions, omitting in some cases the centres, of the ornaments on the ceilings, door-frames, and arches of the old tombs at Delhi. Some of the best of the large ones are taken from the tomb of Homayun, the father of Akbar, who died in A.D. 1556; while the designs for the small series came from the tomb of Khankhanan erected about A.D. 1625.

Some of these salvers are shewn in tho upper parts of the niches and in the top panels of one of the screens in the Metal Court; others, it is proposed, to place on the back walls of several of the Courts.

In the case, which stands in the same bay, a few brass figures have been placed, as well as one or two vessels in which the work is of a more finished character than usual, in order to show what the Hindu artizan is capable of doing.

One of these articles, a Russian Censor, has been carefully copied from a drawing, and is also exhibited as an illustration of the technical skill of tho workmen.

Besides the numerous engraved temple vessels sent from the School of Art, which are arranged in or near Court V, a small collection of sacrificial appliances has been sent. A set of three large lamps, which were made for a temple, is placed on the floor of the Nakarkhana.

A few of tho domestic utensils of the time of the Emperor Akbar have been reproduced from old drawings: these it will be seen are more artistic in shape and ornament than those now in use.

Some of the water-vessels sent are, however, elegant enough, but have been copied from good old designs in the possession of the writer, or from others in the Jeypore Museum, which contains a very large and valuable collection of old brass.

Damascening and Incrustation on Metal.

Throughout Rajputana damascening on metal has been practised from time immemorial. It is chiefly employed to enrich the hilts and mounts of weapons.

In true damascening deep channels are cut into the steel and are filled with gold or silver wire, which is made to adhere by bent and hammering, and then the whole surface is burnished.

Of this work, which is known as *Tah-i-nishan*, several pieces have been contributed by the School of Art, which also sends some trays and other examples of the koft or false damascening to which the design is formed, as at Sealkot in the Punjab, by merely scratching the metal and attaching thin wire, or gold or silver leaf, to it either by hammering or gilding. As in so many other Industries the love of novelty, and the cheapness of the latter methods, have led to their use in preference to the good old-fashioned honest work of the past.

Moreover so great is the demand for damascened arms and ornaments for Europeans, that the artizans find most profit in turning out large quantities of inferior work instead of in concentrating their efforts on the production of a few superior articles, which are only valued by true lovers of art.

Much injury has been done to this, and most indigeeous arts, by the determination of tourists to take away with them from every place they visit specimens of the local manufactures at as cheap a rate as possible, without much regard to whether the article is good or bad. In many places it has thus become almost impossible to secure good work.

A well finished sword hilt covered with panels of flowers or small figures is often a marvel of ingenuity and a thing of beauty, but many of the rusty, uninteresting, and inartistic trinkets and arms sold in or near Sialkot, and latterly at Jeypore, only give rise to the hope that the so-called art may soon become a lost one.

The School of Art also sends some imitations of the special Tanjore work in which silver figures are encrusted on copper.

The crustae are not made in such high relief as those of Tanjore, but a large salver covered with mythological figures is a very fair imitation of the original work.

Arms.

In Rajputana, the home of the Rajputs, the sons of kings, and the representatives of the Kshatriyas, the warrior or second of the great divisions of the Hindu race, is naturally produced every thing that relates to the art of war.

Every Rajput carries a weapon and generally two or three. Of these the sword and *kathar*, or flat dagger, are his national arms, to which in modern times he has added a matchlock or pistol, while formerly a shield was always borne in addition.

Loving his weapon, the mark of his position, and his means of aggression and defence, he best pleases himself by having it ornamented in the most lavish fashion his pocket will permit. Nearly all decorative work in this country was formerly, and in the first instance, applied to arms alone.

H. H. the Maharajah of Jeypore has contributed a few daggers and other weapons, but a large number has not been sent, as it was understood that every form of Indian arm is represented in the South Kensington Museum.

A small collection of modern weapons was purchased by the Royal Commission for decorative purposes, and some of these will probably be shewn in the Jeypore Court, for the industry is one that is characteristic of the State.

There is a large demand by visitors for old arms, consequently they are manufactured for them, that is to say an old blade is fitted to a new handle, or a completely new weapon is made to present a venerable appearance.

Really valuable old arms are exceedingly scarce, and are as much valued by the natives of India as by strangers.

A few shields have been sent. These are made in large numbers as they are still used by the Rajputs, though more as ornaments than for any useful purpose.

CHAPTER X.

PAPIER MACHE MODELS, &c.

IN the fourth Court of the Jeypore series a number of small models
in papier mâché is exhibited. The heads of men of all the principal castes or trades are shown, each wearing the pugri or
turban usually worn by his caste. The visitor will observe that
many of the faces are covered with small pox marks, whilst others
have only one eye due to the ravages of the same fearful disorder
when unchecked by vaccination. The artist has not at all exaggerated
the condition of things in his neighbourhood, where, until the past
twenty years, the disease raged without any attempt to combat it.

In the two sentry boxes on either side of the central avenue, two
full-sized figures in the same material have been placed. The one
on the right represents a *Naja*, or military ascetic, in full dress.
These men live in large numbers in the Jeypore State. They are
celibates and the society is increased by adoption. They live together in large communities and are ruled by a Mahant or abbot.

The native Government pays them a small retaining fee for the
performance of military duties, and in fact these men form the most
faithful soldiers of the State. They lend money and own lands and
are well off as a community.

In the opposite box is the model of a *Chela*, or hereditary servant of
the Maharajah. All Rajput princes and nobles have domestics of this
class born in the house and married in it—retainers who are supported
by their master, and who are faithfully devoted to his interests. A
Rajput would rather starve than see his chelas want, and they in their
turn expect him, not only to feed and clothe them, but to arrange for
their marriages, and for the due performance of all the ceremonies
on their behalf, which are incumbent on a Hindu. The condition
is somewhat similar to serfdom, though, at the present day, there
is nothing to prevent any man in a native State from leaving his

master. Many of these men are wealthy. The word chela means
a disciple as much as a servant. Four models are also sent of the
men who play the musical instruments in the Nakarkhana or
drum-house; and it is intended also to add two representations of
women, who are to lean over the front rail of the drum-house in the
attitude of dropping garlands of flowers upon the heads, or in front
of, distinguished persons who pass beneath. They are copied from
one of the illustrations of the Razmnamah, which was painted in the
time of the Emperor Akbar.

Four smaller figures have also been prepared. These represent
a Rajput and his wife, and a Seth or banker with his wife. They have
all been most carefully dressed and adorned with false jewellery.
In fact all these papier mâché figures are correct studies from
life.

Lacquer Work, &c.

Small wooden articles, such as tobacco or opium boxes and bed-
stead legs, are made in almost every town in Rajputana. They
are turned on a lathe, and lac is applied to them as they are rapidly
revolved in the same instrument. The lac adheres, and is then
polished. In many cases sticks of different colours are employed,
so as to produce the variegated variety of the work, which is most
admired, and is most characteristic of the province.

Khandela, a town in the north of Jeypore, has obtained a great
local reputation for the manufacture of useful lacquered articles, and
at the same place a large quantity of small toys is produced. The
latter are made of wood, which is afterwards painted and covered
with a lac varnish. Small figures of elephants, camels, horses, deer,
and other animals are sold at the rate of about three rupees per
hundred. In the School of Art at Jeypore, a good deal of incised
lacquer is produced. Several coats of lac of different colours are applied one over the other to the articles as they are turned in the lathe,
and figures of different colours are produced by scratching down
to the different layers with sharp tools. It is wonderful with what
rapidity and exactness the artist works in this material. Many of
the animal studies, with which the boxes and vases, such as are
shewn in the School of Art Court, are ornamented, have been taken

from some maces in the private armoury of the Maharajah, two of which are included amongst the exhibits.

One of the most curious articles in the Jeypore collection is a small portable shrine, a copy of one in the Museum, which was in actual use when it was acquired for that institution. The shrine itself contains images of Krishna as Jaganath, of Balrama, and of Subhadra. It is closed by folding doors, which are covered with figures, the whole forming a perfect pantheon ; the paintings are varnished with lac.

In the case in Court VI will be found a number of small boxes in the shape of fruit and of children's toys for making which the material is very suitable.

There is also a considerable collection of lac jewellery. It is incumbent on all married Hindu women to wear lac bracelets, and some of these are very expensively ornamented with turquoises, rubies, or other gems. The patterns with which they are decorated are often very elaborate and artistic.

The bracelet is fastened on the arm when hot, and is worn until it is broken. Covers for native manuscripts are frequently made of wood, on which designs relating to the contents are painted and lacquered, but as these are chiefly interesting on account of the subjects which have been delineated on them, a description of a few will be given in the next chapter.

Betel Nut Carving.

In the sixth Court will also be found a small collection of figures, rulers, walking sticks, and toys, carved from the nut of the *Areca Catechu* or the betel palm. In the same bay some betel leaf boxes, with a water vessel and cup, of *Khus Khus*—Kusa or *Andropogon muriaticus* grass—are exhibited. These articles were made at Kisheogarh, the capital of the Maharajah of a State of the same name in the Jeypore Agency, which is about fourteen miles east of Ajmere.

The grass is fragrant, especially when moist, and is most often used for the manufacture of screens or tatties, which are placed in a window on the side of a room in the hot season. The hot air, in passing through the moistened grass, becomes cool and fragrant.

CHAPTER XI.

PAINTINGS.

A SERIES of small panels, which are used as covers for Jain manuscripts, has been collected, and as the subjects painted upon them are very curious, a short account of them is given here. The numbers are those of the Jeypore Invoice :—

1174.—When Rama brought Sita back from Lanka, where she had been imprisoned by Ravana, he compelled her to undergo the ordeal by fire to purify her from the taint acquired by having lived in a stranger's house.

1175.—A tree loaded with mangoes stood on the way side. A man who was passing by proposed to cut it down to enjoy the fruit at his leisure. His sin was great hence his skin is black. One less wicked thought to lop off a single branch. His degree of iniquity is indicated by his dark blue hue. The third man, who would only break off a twig, is of a light blue colour ; and one who gathered the unripe fruit is red. The sinner, who sat in the tree and ate the ripe fruit, is yellow ; but the pious man, who only picked up that which fell, is of the white or wheaten hue, which all men of high caste or true goodness should be.

1176.—In the next subject a banyan tree represents *life in this world*, while an elephant trying to pull it down is *death*. The two roots, which hang from one of the branches, are the *threads of a single life*, which two mice, *night and day*, are continually gnawing. Between them hangs a mass of honey or *worldly pleasure*, which the man seeks to enjoy, though God from heaven urges him to abandon such dangerous pursuits. He begs for one pleasure more, which turns out to be the last, as the threads are eaten through, and he falls into the pit, where the serpents, avarice, senselessness, desire, and anger, soon destroy him.

1177.—When a Jain lord is about to be born his mother dreams of the fourteen articles represented on this panel. They are—an elephant, a bull, a tiger, the goddess of fortune, garlands, the moon, the sun, the banner of Indra, a kalas or vase, a lotus, the ocean, the vehicle of the gods, a heap of jewels, and a mass of flame without smoke.

1178.—Bahubal, king of Ajodhya, became so firm an ascetic, that creepers grew over his body and snakes hid therein, but he could not attain divine knowledge, as he was still weighted with the care that he stood on ground belonging to his brother, and it was not until his sisters told him that this idea was unbecoming a sage, that he succeeded in his object.

1179.—Rajah Jambu Swami and his wife, after a life of much happiness, determined one night to abandon their riches next day. Some thieves, who were stealing their property in a chamber below them, overheard the discussion, and were so impressed that they also made up their minds to follow their good example, and the whole party became ascetics together.

1180.—Prasanna Chandra, Rajah of Ajodhya, abandoned his throne to become an ascetic. When he was told that his enemies had taken the country from his sons he became angry at being disturbed, for he said " what have I to do with any one but God," and, thus speaking, attained *kewal gyan*, or divine knowledge.

1181.—In his last birth the soul of Rajah Megh Kumar dwelt in the body of an elephant. In a forest fire a little rabbit took refuge under one of the uplifted legs of the huge beast. For six months the noble animal kept his leg up to protect the poor creature from the heat of the raging fire. The limb wasted away and was the cause of the elephant's death, but his soul took fresh birth in the body of a king.

1182.—When the Jain lord attains divine knowledge by which he knows and can describe all things, he is seated on a throne or Samosaran, which Indra, the Lord of Heaven, makes for him, and therefrom he preaches the doctrines of the faith to all creation. The last stage is reached when the ascetic is seated on the tips of his toes, and is very difficult to attain.

1183.—A female saint, whose only food was but a little boiled pulse, fed with it, Mahavira, the 24th Jain Lord, and thus became saved.

1184.—Maru Devi, mother of the first Jain Lord, though quite blind, went to visit her son Rakhabdeo when he attained *kewal gyan* or divine knowledge, and the moment she looked towards him regained her sight.

1185.—Ila, the son of a rich banker, attached himself to a party of Naths or Mountebanks for love of a pretty woman. One day, when balancing himself on a pole in front of a Rajah's house, he saw a pious man next door glancing on the ground as he received alms from a good and lovely lady ; on seeing this he repented and attained divine knowledge.

1186.—Krishna went in great state to Neminath, the 22nd Jain Lord, to pray that he would make his brother Gaj a saint.

1187.—Rajah Srihansa gave sugarcane juice to Rakhabdeo, the first Jain Lord, after he had fasted a month, and thereby attained salvation.

1188.—Gaj Sukh Mal was so lost in mental abstraction, that when his father-in-law put hot ashes on his head he did not feel pain though he was killed by the severe injuries he received. He attained salvation while his enemy was sent to hell.

1189.—Rajah Dasarna once went to revere Mabavira and thought himself the lord of the earth as his following was so great, but the sage humbled his pride by causing Indra to appear in the heavens mounted on his huge elephant in his full pomp as king of gods and men.

1190.—A dove hunted by a sportsman sought asylum with Sagar Chakravarti, a rajah renowned for his charity. When the sportsman, who was the Lord of Heaven in disguise, asked for his lawful prey, the king offered to give an equal weight of his flesh in exchange, but it soon appeared that his whole body would not suffice for the purpose. He thus died and gained salvation.

1191.—Here are represented eight holy objects of devotion, which are always at hand when a Jain Lord is about to be born. They are a mirror, a throne, a vase with eyes, the figure of a maze, a curl or *Srivatsa*, a precious vessel, two fish, and the *Swastica* figure.

1192.—The twenty-four signs of the Jain Lords. These are given on page 18.

1193.—This panel represents the abandonment of the world, and the attainment of beatitude by Dhanna a merchant, and Rajah Sal Bhudra. The former had eight wives and the latter sixty-four, and both were led to adopt this course because the principal wife of the merchant wept on reflecting that all her joy must be at an end when her husband died. This induced him to put an end at once to their trials by abandoning her for the religious life, and the Rajah followed his example.

1194.—The sixteen dreams of Rajah Chandra Gupta, all of which portended evil in the future. They were as follow : -

1. Two elephants fighting without drivers. A sure sign of death.
2. Lotus flowers growing in the sand, indicating that virtue would be neglected.
3. A firefly, who thought that its little light filled the world, showed that small men would become proud.
4. Broken branches of the *Tree of Heaven* implied that vice would increase.
5 & 6. Monkeys riding on elephants, and (No. 6) dogs eating out of golden plates, showed that low persons would sit in high places.
7, 8 & 9. Demons dancing for joy ; (No. 8) the Sun eclipsed ; and (No. 9) the Ocean overflowing its bed, pointed to bad times.
10. Princes riding on camels indicated that they would be reduced to the level of poor men.
11. Holes in the moon (No. 12) and calves yoked in a chariot portended unjust rule, while (No. 13) fish swimming out of the water ; (14) the drying up of the lotuses in a tank ; (15) the gods rising from the earth, and (16) a vision of a serpent with twelve mouths, were signs of fearful gravity.

1212.—This picture represents the counterpart of the story of Joseph and Potiphar's wife except the conclusion, for in the present

instance the end of the impaling instrument by which Seth Sudar-
sana met his death, supported a throne in heaven.

A series of panels on which mythological subjects, relating to the
Brahmanical as well as to the Jain religion, is also exhibited. The
artist who painted them seems to have no limits to the fertility of
his imagination nor to his knowledge of this inexhaustible subject.
The following is a brief account of the pictures :—

1164.—Maha Saraswati, wife of Brahma, Goddess of Speech and
Learning ; Maha Lakshmi, wife of Vishnu, Goddess of
Fortune ; Maha Kali, wife of Siva, Goddess of Destruction.

1165, 1198, 1199, and 1200. The tortures of the damned in hell
where the punishment of each sinner bears some relation
to his crime, as for example, the man, who cuts down a
green tree, is sawn asunder by demons, while birds, snakes,
and wild animals work out their revenge on the bodies of
those who killed or hunted them in the upper world.

1167.—The twenty-four Jain Lords distinguished by a special sign
painted below each sitting figure.

1168.—The ten principal forms of Kali, the great goddess of Bengal.
Our artist was anxious to paint a thousand.

1169.—The nine planets, i.e., the Sun, Moon, Mars, Mercury, Jupiter,
Venus, Saturn, Rahu and Ketu or the ascending and descending nodes which are supposed to cause eclipses.

1170.—The ten Digpalas or the Regents of the ten quarters of
the world, i.e., the eight Cardinal points and the Zenith
and Nadir.

1171.—The twelve months personified.

1172.—The twenty-four Incarnations of Vishnu, the Second person
of the Hindu Trinity.

1173.—The twelve signs of the Zodiac.

1197.—The signs of the 28 lunar Asterisms or Mansions.

1201.—The sixteen *satis* or holy women of the Jains.

1202.—The five great objects of Brahmanical worship.

1203, 1204, 1205, 1211.—Scenes from the Gita Govind or the
sports of Krishna, the Hindu Apollo, and favourite god of
the women.

1206 & 1207.—The personified modes of music.

1208.—Sixteen forms of Durga, the great goddess of Bengal.

1209.—Nine forms of Durga.

1210.—The three great divisions of the day personified.

1212.—The eleven Rudras or manifestations of Siva.

The greatest treasure of the Jeypore family is a copy of the Razmnamah, or Persian abridgment of the Mahabharata, the famous epic poem of the Hindus. The Emperor Akbar ordered a careful translation to be made of this work, which is about seven times as long as Homer, and from it his court poet Sheikh Faizi compiled an abstract. The Emperor hoped that the Hindus might see that many of their superstitions were not supported by their most revered books, whilst the Mahomedans might learn that the world was much older than they thought, and that there was good even in the religion of their fellow subjects.

The Jeypore Razmnamah was in the Imperial library, and of seventeen artists, who lived in Akbar's time, and whose names are recorded in the Ain-i-Akbari or Institutes of Akbar, no less than fourteen were engaged in illustrating this priceless volume. As the drawings were made three centuries ago, when Persian art was at its best, the writer considered, that reproductions of them all would be of great interest to the public, not only as works of art, but because the arms, dress, and accessories delineated in the pictures, are at least those of Akbar's day, and show how little change there has been since then in such matters. He has had photographs of most of the illustrations prepared, and these have been carefully coloured. Copies of the latter have been drawn and painted on wooden panels, which will serve as covers for the Indian Art Journal, or for decorative purposes. The number is so large that it would be impossible to give in a hand-book a detailed description of each plate. A few, however, have been enlarged by a photographic process, and the proper colours carefully painted on the prepared paper. The beauty and truth of the outlines will show how perfectly Akbar's artists did their work, for these cartoons are eight times the size of the originals.

In No. 538 King Yudhishthira is seen escorted by a heavenly guide to the lower world, where he is told the spirits of his brothers are in torment. He starts back as he sees the horrors of this fearful abode, which are most powerfully portrayed in cartoon No. 539. The messenger says that he may return, but at that moment he hears the voices of his relations declaring that his very presence lightens their troubles, and therefore decides to remain for love of them. Immediately the awful vision, for it is but illusion, gives place to sweet fields and beauteous paths, and the shining gods descend to escort him to heaven where he finds his brothers. He has suffered all these horrors because he once failed to speak the whole truth, or had told, what some casuists term, *a lie of necessity.*

In No. 540 we have the birth of Parikshit, the grandson of Arjuna, one of the heroes of the great war. The child was born dead, but Krishna restored it to life.

The picture is full of interest, for all the surroundings of the mother are exactly the same as those that may be seen in any well-to-do Hindu household on a similar occasion at the present day, and the distribution of food and money to beggars outside the gate is equally characteristic. In these respects India has changed but little for many centuries.

541.—At the conclusion of the great war, which is described in the epic, the celebrated sacrifice of a white horse was performed by King Yudhishthira as an atonement for the blood of the Brahmans that had been shed, and as a proof of his universal sovereignty. This interesting rite, in which all the actors were princes, is powerfully delineated,

542.—The white horse was let loose a year before the sacrifice and was allowed to wander whither he willed. If any one molested him, the army of the would-be universal lord fought with the troops of the opposer, and compelled him to yield, and aid their chief in future conflicts. Unless this could be done against all the surrounding chiefs with success, for twelve months, the sacrifice could not be performed.

No. 542 represents the departure of the white horse from Hastienpur the capital.

543.—At the conclusion of the war, the successful party, that is the Pandavas, feasted together. It will be seen in this picture that the women ate separately from the men.

In No. 544, the burning of Lanka, an episode in the Ramayana, the second great Indian epic, which is included in the Mahabharata, is represented. Lanka was ruled by Ravana, a demon king. Hanuman, the monkey god, entered it as a spy but was caught, and his tail, the glory of a monkey, was covered with oiled cloths, and the whole set on fire. Hanuman in revenge increased his size and burnt up one-eighth of the city with his blazing tail.

Platinotypes of all these illustrations have already been published in the "Memorials of the Jeypore Exhibition," and it is proposed to issue a set in colour.

The painting of the wooden panels is very unequal, but the time for preparing them has been so short that the work could not be left in the hands of the best artists only.

The Maharajah of Jeypore has lent from his private library some very fine old paintings. A few of these are of historical value as they include portraits of the Emperors Akbar, Jahangir, Mahomed Shah, and Shah Alum, of Maharajah Madho Sing I. of Jeypore, in green or hunting dress, of Prince Dara Shikoh, son of Shah Jahan, and of Mirza Hindol, brother of the Emperor Humayun; small copies of some full size contemporary portraits of the Maharajahs of Jeypore are also contributed. In the originals the ornaments worn by the chiefs are shown in relief. The frames have doors, which close in the style of venetian dyptichs.

As Jeypore is celebrated for its mythological paintings a few of the more finished examples are exhibited (Nos. 570 to 580). The common bazar pictures give a good idea of native life and of the style of art which is most appreciated by the inhabitants of India. Amongst the contributions will be found a series of portraits of men and women of most of the common castes and occupations (Nos. 582 to 616). Representations of the great processions, or of the Mystery plays for which Jeypore is famous (Nos. 617 to 621), and a small set of drawings, in which all the ceremonies attendant upon the birth of a Rajput, are shewn (Nos. 1745 to 1763.)

CHAPTER XII.

TEXTILES.

THE most interesting, and most characteristic amongst Jeypore textiles, are the Sanganir and Bagroo Chiotzes or dyed and stamped cotton cloths.

These are made at small towns situated respectively at seven and eighteen miles from Jeypore on branches of the Amanisha stream, which drains the hills near Jeypore, and supplies the city with water.

The peculiar hue of the cloth, the well known and admired *couleur d'ivoire*, is produced by repeated washings of the fabric in this river.

Country-cloth is used by the dyers and has been employed for the large collection of patterns sent to the Exhibition, but English Calicoes have for many years past almost driven the local material out of the market. There is now, however, a reaction in its favour owing to the inferiority of the imported oversized cloth.

Sanganir, the chief seat of this manufacture, is a most picturesque little town with a richly carved marble Jain temple, some 900 years old. It is said that the chintz printers have been established here for from ten to fifteen generations, and that the art was introduced from Panderpur in Gujerat, where Namdeo, the patron of the craft, was first taught it by revelation. He is now worshipped at Sanganir and Bagroo.

All the printers are Hindus; they are very superstitious, and make a point of once or twice a year visiting the great temple at Jeypore of Ganesh, the god whose vehicle is a rat, to implore him to protect their cloths from being eaten by his subjects, the rats and mice.

Their manufacturing processes are of the rudest description.

They first wash the white cloth in the water of the river, and then

D

immerse it in a solution of sesamum oil, water, and *khar*, a saline efflorescence obtained from the banks of the stream. The cloth is then dried in the sun, and the oil and impurity removed by immersion in a solution of goat's dung and water many times, and by washing in pure water. When clean it is dipped in a solution of Har or *Terminalia chebula*, a vegetable mordaunt, and again dried.

The outlines of the patterns are then applied with an ink composed of alum, turmeric, sulphate of iron, madder (*Rubia cordifolia*) *Grislea tomentosa* flowers and a little oil.

After the printing, which is done with wooden blocks, the cloths, if the ground is to be red, are boiled in a solution of Al or *Morinda citrifolia*, Madder, and Myrobalans, or Har, and dried.

The last process is the washing in the river, and it is a very picturesque sight as one approaches the town to see the banks of the stream, which flows beneath its old walls, covered with prints of all kinds spread out to dry.

The designs are prepared by Joypore artists, and the blocks to produce them are cut by several families of Mahomedan workmen, whose ancestors came from Mooltan. A collection of these blocks, which are cut from several hard woods, is exhibited.

A few very fine chintzes, made some 60 or 70 years ago, are also shewn. They are the property of the Maharajah, and were especially made for one of his ancestors, as it was the custom for the chief to wear new patterns of Sanganir cloths some months before the general public were allowed to use them.

The patterns were frequently changed, and thus there was a constant demand for these interesting and artistic fabrics, the production of which is injured by the machine-made imitations, which are turned out by the mile from the factories of Manchester.

One firm, finding that its cloths were too regular in design for the Jeypore taste, has even succeeded in copying the imperfections of the local fabrics.

About three thousand different patterns have been especially prepared for the Exhibition. Most of these have been made from old stamps, some of which have been in the possession of the printers for two hundred years.

The chintzes are worn throughout Rajputana and the neighbouring districts, and, as the colours are bright and harmonious, on the days, when fairs are held, or always in the evening in the main streets of Jeypore, the crowd presents a gay and picturesque appearance very different from the sombre hue of the dress of the people who throng the cities of the Punjab or even the North-West Provinces. The Sanganir and Bagroo cloths, which are very like them, are admirably adapted for decorative purposes as well as for personal wear, and the demand for them amongst Europeans is increasing. The patterns on the dark green, and light yellow cloths, are frequently stamped with gold or silver leaf, and, as will be seen from a few examples contributed to the Exhibition, with excellent effect. Cloths stamped with false metal are not much used in Jeypore and are rarely made.

In fact in former days in native Courts, the use of false metal for all such purposes, including the manufacture of lace and spangles for ornamenting shoes, was discouraged by fines.

A large number of Mahomedans are engaged in the dye trade in the capital. The colours they use are generally non-permanent, but in the eyes of the inhabitants of Rajputana, and especially of Jeypore, the city of brightness and pleasure, this is no demerit. It is customary for the whole community to appear at the different festivals in different colours. Thus one day every one may wear red, the next green, and on another pink clothing. It is often alleged by them as a reason for using the *new* aniline colours, or *naya pang*, that cloth dyed with them can be easily redyed another hue when the first has served its turn and thus expense be saved.

The fashions are constantly changing, as for example, small handkerchiefs, dyed with geometrical and floral patterns, in yellow ochre have lately been much sold amongst all classes (Nos. 1881—1892). Some cloths for petticoats, dyed in fast colours, are also sent. These are sold all over Rajputana, and as widows are not allowed to wear cloths dyed with non-permanent hues, there is a ready sale for them (Nos. 1868—1872).

The pagries or turbans on the papier mâché heads in Court IV give a good idea of a manufacture which is much admired. The waved or *Lahriya* pattern is most used for those articles and many colours are introduced.

Susis or striped cotton cloths (Nos. 1842—1860) are made for the trowsers of Mahomedan women.

The Bandhuna or tied cloths also find a large sale. The pattern is produced by knotting up with thread any portion of the cloth which is to escape being dyed. For each of the many colours required to produce an elaborate design, a separate knotting is required, and the labor involved is enormous, though the skill and rapidity with which the work is done by tho women is marvellous. Peacocks and animals, thus built up of different coloured dots, are much in demand. In all these industries the women and even children take as important a part as the men, and the visitor cannot help being struck by the healthiness, cheerfulness, and happiness of all engaged in them—a sad contrast with the miserable appearance of the operatives in manufacturing towns in Europe or even in Bombay.

Much is said of the terrible lot of women in India, but it is certain that the wives of the handicraftsmen in the textile and many other industries, while taking their fair share of the toil, have fully as much enjoyment, and very little less power than their lords. Their ways are different from ours, but they have many pleasures, which Europeans in tho same class in life do not possess. Amongst these are the many fairs which are held in the Spring and Autumn, the marriages and feastings at which the women assist, though generally apart from the men, and the constant promenading in gay dresses through the streets in parties, who sing songs together.

The work of a cloth-dyer and printer is quite a family affair. The young men do tho rough work, the women and children apply the stamps, and the old people sort the chintzes or bargain with the baneahs or dealers, who sell them in the bazar or market.

Amongst the wooden blocks will be found a few which are used in pairs for stamping raised patterns on the borders of the white clothing used by the better classes of Mahomedans. Every time the garment is washed it is ornamented in this way by the women of the family.

Fells.

The town of Malpura, about sixty miles south-west of Jeypore, has obtained more than a local reputation for the manufacture of *Namdah* or felt.

. Wool is well washed with soap and water, and dried. Thin layers are then spread out on cloths, and, after saturation with soap and water, are felted by being beaten with a thin stick. Layer after layer is added to produce the required thickness.

In all probability the Art was introduced, through the Mahomedans of Delhi, from Persia where it is well known. Specimens of the chief forms into which it is worked are exhibited at the back of Court II. It will be seen that coloured pieces are introduced with good effect in some articles. No. 1932 is a *Googy*, or cape with a hood, which is worn throughout Rajputana as a waterproof cloak in the rainy season.

. No. 1938 is a round Hindu prayer rug or *Asin*, which is used by Brahmans and Rajputs when engaged in their religious devotions.

Nos. 1935 and 1937 are Mahomedan Prayer Carpet in (Jal-ea-mar) in which a small niche-shaped pattern is made. The apex of the niche should point to Mecca, and, in the case of the strict Sheah sect, upon it is placed a small piece of the sacred soil of Karbela—for the forehead should touch the earth every time the worshipper prostrates himself.

No. 1929 is a Gun or Matchlock Cover for use in the rainy season.

Nos. 1930 and 1931 are saddle *Namdahs*, for which there is a large demand in native cavalry regiments.

Nos. 1933 and 1934 are *Chackmas*, or floor cloths, which in Persia are placed at the sides and top of a room.

No. 1936 is a square Prayer Carpet also used by the *Hindus.*

Cotton Floor Cloths, Woollen Rugs and Carpets.

. Cotton floor cloths or *durries* are chiefly made in Jails, and samples of these in which bright colours have been introduced, are sent from the Jeypore Central Prison.

From the same institution are forwarded some woollen rugs and two small carpets, which are adaptations or copies of some magnificent old examples belonging to the Jeypore State.

As those old fabrics have been freely lent to the Lahore, Agra, Ajmere and other Jails, and as it is understood that a few reproductions of these are being exhibited, a short account of the originals will not be out of place here.

It was generally supposed at Jeypore that the large collection of carpets, which belonged to the State, had been brought as spoils of war from Herat about 300 years ago by Maharajah Man Singh, who was Governor of Cabul, but recent researches have led to the discovery of a number of these beautiful fabrics in the old capital at Amber, and these each bear a label in which the price, size, date, and place of manufacture are given.

It appears that these carpets were made to order in Lahore more than 248 years ago, and as Abul Fazl, Akbar's historian, clearly states that there was a factory at this place, which produced carpets exceeding in beauty those of Persia, there is no reason to doubt the truth of the above, though there is still evidence that some at least of the Jeypore carpets came with Maharajah Man Singh. The following extract from the writer's work on the Jeypore exhibition will give some idea of the special beauties of these works of art :—

"Although these splendid fabrics have been in use nearly three "hundred years, many of them show but little trace of decay. Age "has given them a richness of tone and harmony which has greatly "improved their appearance, though it is almost impossible to believe "that they were ever lacking in these respects.

"The patterns are very varied. They are always bold and graceful, "and although continuity of design is preserved, no two parts of the "same carpet, however large it may be, quite resemble each "other.

"The borders of the Jeypore carpets are invariably darker than "the centres, and the corner patterns are carefully blended—a point "not always attended to in modern work. There are a few geometrical "designs, but in most of the examples leaves and flowers stand out "from a rich rosy red or indigo-blue ground. The bent rose leaf, "which in Indian Jails has degenerated into the fish pattern, the "conventional Tartar cloud, in its simplest form, or arranged as an

" escutcheon of interlacing clouds, and the great shield pattern, are
" most commonly seen. The gem of the collection is a pair of rugs
" with a common border similar to a double Cashmere shawl. The
" centre of each compartment represents a verdant meadow full
" of birds, beasts, fishes, and monsters of strange forms and
" colours."

A well-finished, careful, copy, on the scale of two inches to a foot,
of this wonderful carpet has been made by Goberdhan, the Artist
to the Jeypore Museum, and is contributed to the Exhibition as
an example, not only of the beauty of the fabrics, but of the patient
skill of the copyist.

A smaller rug from the Jail, the pattern of which has been taken
from one of the frescoes in the Ajonta caves, and a coloured drawing
of a quarter of another old rug, on the scale of three inches to the
foot, are also sent.

CHAPTER XIII.

MODELS.

ALTHOUGH a few remarks have already been made on a previous page regarding some of the models, it is desirable to draw special attention to the subject, for some of them are of great interest.

437.—*Stone Shrine.* This is a full sized copy of one in actual use in one of the principal streets of Jeypore. In the centre in the original is placed the llogam or emblem of Siva, and around, and facing it, are Parvati his wife, Ganesh his son the elephant-headed God of Wisdom, and Nandi the bull on which he is supposed to ride, the whole forming a *dewugan* or Court of Gods. There are many such shrines in the centres and on the side parements of the principal streets in Jeypore, and towards evening lights are placed in them, and many persons step aside from the crowd and worship before them.

419.—*Shrine of Garuda.* This is a model on a small scale of a Kiosk for the demigod Garuda, the Vulture King, or the vehicle of the God Vishnu. The original stands before the temple of Jagat Siromani at Amber, a remarkable building inasmuch as it is not unlike a Christian Church with spire, naive, side aisles, chancel, organ loft, and galleries.

The struts, which support the arches, are very similar to those employed in the celebrated Jain temples at Mount Aboo, from which the idea may have been taken, as the Kiosk is only about 300 years old, or 600 years less than the former. The architecture, more especially the ornament on the plinth, is a good example of the Chalukya style of Fergusson.

417.—*Model in brass of the Cenotaph of Maharajah Sawai Jey Singh, the founder of Jeypore.* This beautiful building is constructed of pure white marble, and stands in a garden in a quiet valley under the fort of Jeypore. Around it are many other charming cenotaphs of the Chiefs of Jeypore. Though none are so beautiful as this, yet each has its peculiarities, especially in the mode in which the dome springs from its octagonal base.

Two full-sized panels in marble from the plinth of Jey Singh's cenotaph will afford an idea of the way in which the whole building is finished (Nos. 137-138), but the brass work, though minute, is so skilfully executed that it was perhaps unnecessary to send these plaques.

Under one of the little Kiosks at the corner of the platform on which the cenotaph stands, a light is kept perpetually burning to the memory of the departed head of all the Kachwaha Rajputs, who was a real King amongst men.

420.—*Model of a gateway in brass, gilt, and coloured.* A full description of this will be found at page 19.

The next six exhibits are models of vehicles, which are in common use throughout the Rajput States. They were made in the Jeypore State workshops.

No. 421.—The *Baili* is generally employed by all classes in the country districts, as well as by merchants, bankers and officials in the towns. A pair of fine bullocks from Nagore in Marwar, a famous breed, is generally preferred both for the *Baili* and for the *Rath*.

No. 422.—The *Rath*, the conveyance of the higher classes, and of women. This is a luxurious carriage, picturesque in appearance, and not at all uncomfortable over sandy roads.

No. 423 is a *Mahadol* or palki used in marriages, in processions for a bride and bridegroom, and also by priests.

No. 424.—The *Takht Rawan*, or portable throne, is employed on grand occasions when the chief or an image is carried in procession. The silver parcel gilt work on this specimen is very good.

No. 425 is a model of the ordinary palki used in Bengal, and No. 426 is a small *Tamjham* or portable seat most frequently used in the interior of palaces for crossing Courts or for ascending to forts.

State Paraphernalia.

Morchals or fly-whisks. These are carried by State servants behind their master, and are made of peacock's feathers enriched with gold. Besides the two which have been sent to London, a small collection, showing the different modes of ornamenting the eyes of the feathers with gold wire and spangles, is contributed, and there is also a pair of imitation *morchals* which are used by religious beggars in mockery of human state.

Chamaras, Chanries, or fly whisks. These are also carried behind princes; they are made up of from two to five or more tails of the yak or *Bos grunniens,* and are mounted on handles of gold, silver, or plated metal, which are sometimes enriched with enamel and precious stones.

A State *Ankash* or elephant goad has not been sent.

Mahi maratib or the symbol of nobility given by the Moghul Emperors to great nobles. This is described at page 15.

Panch Ranga or banner of five colours. The stripes are horizontal, but there is no fixed order of arrangement. The standard is not peculiar to Jeypore, but the one in use in that State is usually surmounted by a smaller one, a fourth its size, on the same pole, as the chief possesses the title of "Sawai," which indicates that his ancestor was a *quarter* better than any other prince in the estimation of the Mogul Sovereign who gave it to him.

Delhi Assemblage Banner. This is a small copy of the standard that was given to His Highness the late Maharajah of Jeypore, when H. M. the Queen assumed the title of Empress of India. His arms, which were devised a few years ago, are displayed on one side of it. The flag was embroidered and sewn by young women and girls in the State Female Schools under the superintendence of Miss Joyce, under whom also the *Aftabi* or *Adani* was matter.

The *Aftabi* is a sunshade, and the one exhibited is a fine specimen of needle work and embroidery. On one side is the Sun, on the other the Moon, the fabled ancestors of the two great divisions of the Rajput race, and round them revolve Krishna and the *gopis* or milkmaids, symbolical of the Heavenly Zodiac.

The *Chattar* or umbrella (not exhibited) is usually of a bright red colour.

The musical instruments in the *Nakarkhana. Naubat* or large drums; *Nakaras* or kettle-drums; *Karnaul* or *Bhumbhara,* a long horn or trumpet of metal; *Surna* or *sarnai*, a small flute; *Jkanj* or *sanj*, a pair of cymbals.

The *Shamianah* or canopy of the throne, which is richly embroidered, and supported on poles of silver.

The throne or *Takt* upon which is the *gaddâ* or cushion of Hindu Sovereignty.

The *Takt Rawan* or portable throne, the *Mahadol* and *Rath*, are state vehicles.

Alam, a lance of bamboo with a tuft of black wool or hair near the top.

Some of these articles have been omitted owing to want of space.

Observatory.

To justly estimate the great services rendered to astronomy by Maharajah Sawai Jey Singh, the position of the science at the same period in England should be considered.

When Flamsteed, the first astronomer royal at Greenwich, died on December 31st, 1719, his famous observations, entitled Historia Coelestis Britannica (a copy of which work, now in the Jeypore Library, was obtained by Jey Singh) were yet unpublished. The only instruments possessed by Flamsteed were an iron sextant of six feet radius, two clocks, a three-feet quadrant, two telescopes, and a mural arc. He established the obliquity of the ecliptic and the position of the equinox. [*]

Jey Singh ascertained the former with the mural quadrant or *Bhitti Yantr* which he constructed.

Dr. Holley, who succeeded Flamsteed, had only a small transit instrument, and afterwards an eight-feet mural quadrant; and Bradley, who followed him in 1742, about the last year of Jey Singh's life, for seven years had but one instrument more—A zenith sector of twelve feet radius. The facts above stated cannot but reflect the greatest credit on the memory of the ruler, who at a period when his highest powers, as a general and politician, were demanded to preserve the very existence of his state, was yet so devoted to science as to found five great observatories, and to fill them, not only with the

---

[*] The date of the first observation in Greenwich Observatory was Sept. 19th, 1676.

Instruments known to his countrymen, but was so enlightened as to send to far distant countries for works bearing on the grand science to which he devoted his talents, and to seek assistance from European scholars. The Observatory at Benares has often been described because that city is on the usual route followed by travellers. There is also an excellent description, by Hunter, of the Delhi Observatory, in the fifth Volume of the Asiatic Society's Researches published in 1797. The principal Institution at Jeypore has, however, not attracted so much attention. With the view, therefore, of adequately representing the state of astronomical science in India in Jey Singh's time, careful models have been prepared for the exhibition of the instruments contained in it. Maharajah Sawai Jey Singh, at the request of the Emperor Mahomed Shah, reformed the Calendar. In the Zee-ji-Mahomed Shahi, a new set of tables which he prepared, the prince gives as his reasons for constructing huge instruments of solid stone and lime, the inaccuracy of the ancient brass instruments (a few of which are exhibited) due to the smallness of their size, the want of division into minutes, the shaking of their axles, the displacement of the centres of the circles, and the shifting of their planes. He adds that he constructed instruments at different places to confirm the truth of the observations made at Delhi, and that having heard that observatories had been built in Europe by the learned, he had sent skilful persons with Padre Manuel to see what was being done there and to obtain the new tables published by De La Hire. He finished his own tables in A. D. 1728.

The Observatory at Jeypore is within the Palace enclosure. It is a large square surrounded by walls and buildings, many of which were not in existence in Jey Singh's time.

The positions of the different Instruments are shewn on the plan. They have been modelled to the scale of one inch to two feet, and the graduations have been carefully marked.

The following is a brief description of each instrument. The numbers refer to the plan :—

1.—*Vustr Samrat.* The prince of dials. This is probably the largest sundial in the world as its gnomon is 89 feet high. As it is exactly like the small dial (No. 10) or *Narivalay*,

PLAN OF THE JEYPORE OBSERVATORY.

Showing the relative position of the instruments

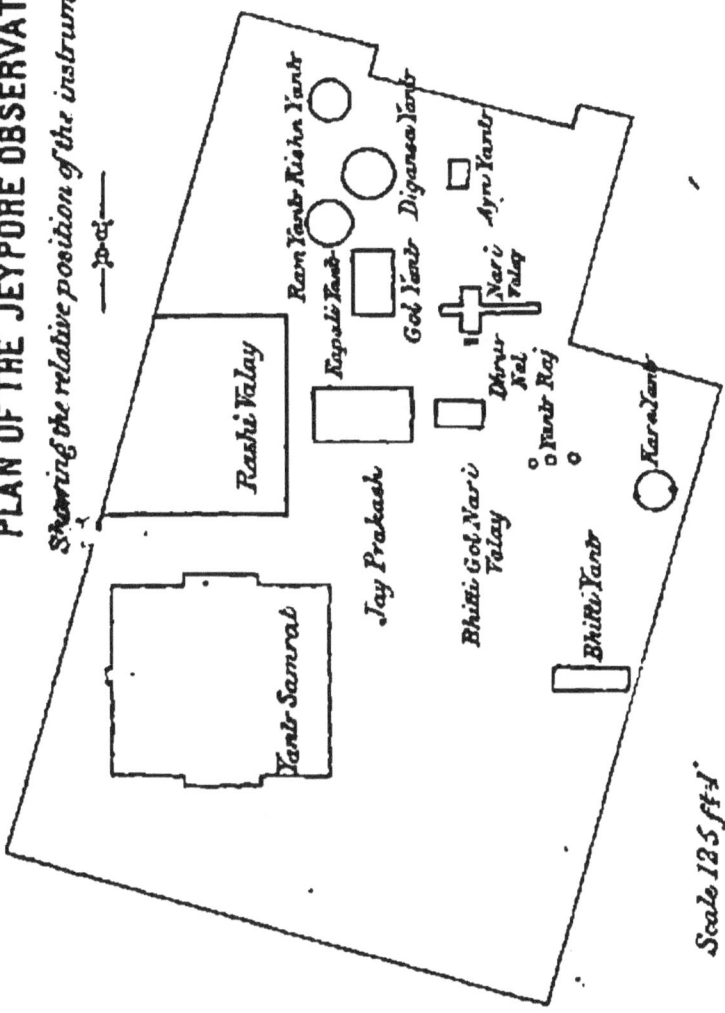

Rashi Walay

Ram Yantr Kishn Yantr

Kapali Yantr

Gol Yantr

Digansa Yantr

Ayn Yantr

Nari
Walay

Dhruv
Wl.
Yantr Raj

Jay Prakash

Yantr Samrat

Bhitti Gol Nari
Walay

Kara Yantr

Bhitti Yantr

N

Scale 125 ft.

Calcutta Central Press Co. Ld

the description of that instrument will be sufficient. It has also been decided not to send it to Europe.

2.—*Bhitti yantr.* Double mural quadrant. The sun's altitude and zenith distance at noon, his greatest declination, the obliquity of the ecliptic and the latitude of Jeypore can be found with this instrument.

3.—*Rashivalay.* A zodiacal dial made up of twelve small dials each of which is used when the sun is in a particular sign. The moment of true noon can thus be found at any time of the year.

4.—*Yantr Jai Prakash.* A pair of concave cups, complimentary to each other, which represent the inferior hemisphere of the heavens.

5.—*Bhitti gol nari yantr.* A double equinoctial dial. With this instrument the time may be determined when the sun is either in the northern or southern signs, and the declination may also be found; similar observations may be made on the stars.

6.—*Yantr Raj.* Two large metal plates by which the declination of the stars or planets, and many other data, may be determined.

7.—*Kura Yantr or Chakr yantr.* A large altitude circle.

8.—*Kapali Yantra.* Two cups shaped like the vault of the skull used for making a great variety of observations.

9.—*Gol Yantr.* With this instrument the time of eclipses can be ascertained.

10.—*Narivlay.* A sundial.

11.—*Druv Nal.* Pointer to the North Pole.

12.—*Ram Yantr.*

13.—*Krishn Yantr.* These two instruments, which are complimentary to each other are used to ascertain the sun's azimuth by the shadow of a central pillar on the walls, and his altitude by the shadows cast on the horizontal radii.

14.—*Dig ansa Yantr or Shanro Yantr.* An azimuth instrument.

15.—*Ayn Yantr.* A north equinoctial dial.

Five of the old small brass instruments which Maharajah Jey Singh used are also lent to the Exhibition.

454.—A long brass portable dial with which the time and other data may be ascertained by means of a pointer.

455.—A similar one of wood.

456, 457 and 458. Three portable instruments known as the Yantr Raj. These are still in use for calculating the heights of buildings, trees, &c., as well as the altitude of the stars or sun and moon.

Photographs.

The art of Photography is one admirably adapted to the capacities of the natives of India. They are patient and have tho artistic sense well developed. Some of their work is very superior, and Lalla Din Dayal of Indore, a number of whose views is contributed, has secured several gold medals at exhibitions, as well as high praise for his love for the art, in studying which he spares neither time nor money.

A selection of his views of Jeypore, and the neighbourhood, has been made, and tinted by the best local artists, in order that the public may be able to judge the better of the beauty and interest of the scenery and buildings which he has depicted, for experience has shewn that a series of uncoloured photographs is not likely to attract much attention.

The numbers given on the views are those of the photographer,[*] who can supply untinted duplicates if these figures are quoted. Special attention may be drawn to the following :—

1769-1770.—Panoramic view of the main street of Jeypore.

1810.—The procession of the Sun in the Amber Square.

1808.—The Palace of the Wind, Jeypore.

1805.—Great Gate of the Palace, Jeypore.

1783.—The principal Tank in the Galta Pass, Jeypore.

1791.—Cenotaph of Maharajah Jey Singh, at Gehtore, near Jeypore.

1774.—Embankment of the tank at Amber, the old capital.

1764.—Grand entrance to the principal apartments, Amber Palace.

1796, 1796a.—Panoramic view of Amber.

1776.—The temple of Jagat Seromani, Amber.

Mr. Green, a Bengali native Christian, the Photographer to H. H. the Maharajah of Jeypore, has also taken a number of excellent views of places and buildings in the Jeypore State.

---

[*] Agent of Lalla Din Dayal, Mr. H. Farrar, 6, Hanway St., London, W.

The following are of importance in connection with remarks made in this handbook :—

885.—Jain Altar at Sanganir.

888.—Another view of the Jain Altar.

890.—The Town of Chatsu.

900.—Palace at Toda Rai Singh, Jeypore.

907.—A Garnet Mine near Dunl, Jeypore.

909.—The Banas river at Bisalpore.

910.—The Banas river at Rajmahal.

913.—The fort of Ranthambhor.

917 and 918. Views of Sawai Madhopore.

930.—Shekhawati carvers, including a portrait of a little boy, one of the best workmen.

933.—Town of Malpura.

939 to 943.—The Sambhur Lake and Salt Works.

944—The Deoyani Tank at Sambhur.

A few portraits of Khetri retainers, the work of Yusuf Ismail, photographer to the Rajoh of Khetri, have also been sent.

CHAPTER XIV.

MORAL AND MATERIAL PROGRESS SINCE THE BRITISH CONNECTION WITH JEYPORE.

READERS of Indian history are well acquainted with the utterly prostrate condition into which the Rajput States had fallen at the beginning of the present century. Jeypore especially lay almost at the mercy of the Mahrattas, and their ally the first Nawab of Tonk, whose troops, at the close of every rainy season, set out literally to live in the surrounding districts, systematically quartering themselves upon, or robbing, every town and village within reach.

. Under such circumstances it can easily be understood that there were no made roads, that irrigation works on a large scale were abandoned, that manufactures were not encouraged, and that education, art, and science were almost in abeyance. The Marquis of Wellesley concluded a treaty with the Maharajah of Jeypore in 1803, but the alliance was dissolved shortly afterwards, and was not renewed until April 1818, when a new treaty was made. Although the good influence of the British Government was immediately felt in the restoration of proper relations between Jeypore and its great nobles and feudatories, it was not until the reign of Maharajah Ram Singh, which began in 1835, that there was much improvement in the administration and in the general condition of the population.

A Regency Council was appointed in 1839-40 and according to Col. Brooke—" In no native State in India had so many great and beneficial measures been inaugurated in so short a time, as were introduced by the Jeypore Council of Regency." Enactments were issued against Sati, and laws made against Infanticide, slavery, exactions of Bhats and Charans on the occasion of marriages, etc.

Much of the above account has been summarized from a little work by Dr. Stratton, late Resident at Jeypore, and the writer cannot do better than to quote his notice in the first place of the improvements made by the late Chief Maharajah Sawai Ram Singh II, and then of those of the present ruler Maharajah Sawai Madho Singh II, who succeeded in September 1880.

Public Works.

"This department was started about 1860 under Colonel Price; and has since 1867 been under Lieutenant-Colonel S. S. Jacob, the Executive Engineer of the State.

"Up to the death of the late Maharajah in September 1880 some 49 lakhs of rupees had been spent on roads, tanks, and buildings, besides several lakhs more under a separate Imarat or State Works Office. Of roads constructed, the principal is the Agra and Ajmere highway, now somewhat superseded by the Railway, which bisects the State, forking at Bandikui for Agra and Delhi and at Phalera for Ajmere and Sambhur, &c.

" Irrigation works, including those constructed under the present Chief, number above 100, large and small, capable of irrigating some 32,000 acres. The area in square miles of the larger lakes is, of Tori, just completed 6½; Kalak, 2½; Mora, 2; Khur, 1½; and Buchara, nearly finished, 1½.

" Projects are ready for still larger reservoirs on the Banganga at Jamwa—Ramgarh, and the Banas on the Ajmere frontier.

" City water-works started in 1872 and opened in 1875. The water is pumped by steam engines from the Amanisha stream into a high level reservoir, whence it flows in pipes to the city with free taps in all the streets.

"*City Gas Works.* Started in 1878. Gas at first was made from castor, but now from kerosine oil, in the manufacture from which sundry improvements have been made by Mr. S. J. Tellery in charge under Col. Jacob. Streets and main roads lighted free.

"*Albert Hall in the Public Gardens.* Foundation laid by H. R. H. The Prince of Wales. Intended for Public Hall, and Museum. A large and handsome structure, with much beautiful carved marble work, which Col. Jacob has had designed and adapted from the finest examples of old Indian stone carving. Not yet completed. Will cost some five lakhs.

E

"*Mayo Hospital*, designed by Dr. DeFabeck, also in the gardens. Foundation laid by Lord Mayo.

"*Mayo Statue* in the gardens. Bronze, by Forsyth, a duplicate of that at Cockermouth. Erected by the late Maharajah in memory of his friend. Unveiled by Lord Northbrook.

"*Ram Newas Public Gardens*. Area 76 acres. Site chosen by late Chief to be near the city and thus convenient to the people. Besides the Albert Hall, Mayo Hospital and Mayo Statue, there are good Zoological collections of beasts and birds.

Medical Institutions.[*]

"The Medical Department of the State was first started on a small scale in the time of the late Chief's minority, since which it has gradually developed until now, when, including some new Dispensaries established under the present Maharajah, it comprises one first class institution, the Mayo Hospital at the capital, and 21 other dispensaries and hospitals throughout the territory, of which latter class five are supported by Feudatories. Vaccination was started in 1870, and last year there were 53,173 children vaccinated. In 1885 no less than 88,326 patients were treated.

Education.

"The Maharajah's Collegiate, Jeypore, was founded in 1844. The languages taught are English, Hindi, Urdu, and Persian. Teaches up to First Arts' standard of Calcutta University, and has over 1,000 students.

"The Sanscrit College founded in 1865. Number of students, 217.

"The Rajput School for sons of Nobles. Founded in 1862. Scholars 33.

"The Girls School with several branches. Founded in 1867. Scholars in all 556. Under the Misses Joyce.

"The State Schools in the Districts number 44 with over 1,000 pupils, besides other aided and indigenous schools.

"The Public Library and Reading Room. Established in 1866.

"Many examples of needle work and embroidery, the work of the pupils of the Girls' School, have been contributed to the Exhibition. These institutions are now under Baboo Dinanath Mukerji."

---

* Under Surgeon Major Hendley, Agency Surgeon.

Science and Art.

"Ever since the time of the Astronomer Prince, Sawai Jey Singh, something of Science and Art has lingered at Jeypore, but this is now having a richer development.

"The late Chief established a small Meteorological Observatory, but unfortunately under circumstances preventing full success; and also a Natural History Museum, but finding this not answer expectations he abolished it. The Observatory and Museum, now existing, date thus from the present Chief's time as hereafter noticed.

"A School of Art was established by the late Chief in 1866, under Dr. DeFabeck, and for the last ten years it has been under a native principal, Baboo Opendro Nath Sen. Drawing, designing and most sorts of Art work in metal and pottery, &c., &c., are taught.

"Taste or ability in Art is inborn or bred by long training, and is not to be summarily created, but there is no doubt the school has in its time done good work and diffused better knowledge among workmen, so that articles, once a speciality of the school manufacture, are now made and sold in the ordinary bazar, while lads, after being versed in simple drawing, become apt draftsmen and designers, when brought under the advanced practical training of Col. Jacob's Architectural Department."

In Court No. V, most of the contributions of the School of Art have been arranged.

The articles were selected by the Principal of the School.

During the time of the present Maharajah the following improvements have been made :—

"Transit duties have now been entirely abolished on all articles, except opium and other intoxicants." Those who have read the travels of Bernier, Tavernier and others in the 17th and 18th centuries, when every petty noble levied a tax, can appreciate the immense relief to trade of such a concession.

Two educated native women have been sent, at the cost of the State, to learn medical work at the Female Medical School at Agra.

Students have been sent to the Punjab to learn district work as conducted in British territory ; others are being trained, at Rurki, as Engineers, and, at Dehra Dun, as Forest Rangers.

A Forest Officer, whose services were lent by the Imperial Government, has surveyed the forests.

The garnet industry has been developed, and no less than 37 lakhs of rupees have been devoted to Public Works. In this period some of the largest irrigation works before noticed have been undertaken.

"Irrigation pays both State and cultivator, and is therefore very popular—a result mainly due to the care of Col. Jacob, the Engineer, for the interests of all parties."

A steam Hydraulic Cotton Press has also been erected.

"The Meteorological Instruments provided by the late Maharajah were in 1881, at the suggestion of the Agency Surgeon, placed in a suitable position, and supplemented by others, with a staff of trained observers attached, under the supervision of the officer just named.

"The principal instrument in the original set was an Osler's improved Anemograph ; but in 1882 was added a Van Rysselberghe's Meteorograph, a wonderfully delicate complex, automatic instrument. It is one of two in this country, but the only one as yet in regular working.

"The Institution is now an observatory of the first class, and sends daily telegrams to our Meteorological Department.

"Though the old Natural History Museum was abolished by its founder the late Chief, the need was soon felt of another of a different sort, viz., an Economic and Industrial Museum ; and this also was started in 1881, at the suggestion of the Agency Surgeon. The natives have thoroughly taken to it, more than 1½ millions having visited it since its opening.

"In the beginning of 1883 an Industrial and Art Exhibition was held at Jeypore supported by the liberality of His Highness the Maharajah. The visitors numbered over a quarter of a million."

A series of maps has been especially coloured in illustration of the above remarks."

No. 2090 shows the irrigation works, land irrigable from them, metalled and fair-weather roads, the railway, and the old Moghul, road marked by the Cos Minars or milestones of the Emperors of Delhi.

No. 2091 shows the length and drainage area of the rivers and lakes.

No. 2092 gives the Imperial and Jeypore State postal lines, the populations of the principal towns at the last census, the capitals of *Nizamuts* or provinces (marked by a red circle), and the dispensary towns marked by a blue circle.

No. 2093 is a geological map of the State.

A complete series of all the printed annual and special reports of the Public Works, the Medical, and Educational Departments, and of the School of Art with specimens of caligraphy from the College are also sent.

The Rev. S. Macalister, of the United Presbyterian Mission at Jeypore, has also collected some educational appliances in use in native schools. There are two European Missionaries, besides two Zenana ladies, catechists, readers, teachers, and assistants, who had in 1885 on their school rolls 783 boys. Through the Rev. J. Traill, of the above Mission, a copy of the Bani or Holy Book of the Dadu Panthis, of which sect the Nagas or military ascetics are members, has been secured.

Raw Produce Collection.

A raw produce collection has not been sent as this section was undertaken by the Revenue and Agricultural Department of the Government of India.

APPENDIX I.

ARRANGEMENT OF THE JEYPORE COURTS.

SCREEN B—
Jeypore tiles in the upper panels and two pictures in the same material in niches below.

1. The great gate of the men's apartments, Amber Palace.
2. The Chandra Mahal, or Palace of the Moon, Jeypore.

BACK WALL—
1. Marble window.
2. A large Brass Tray, old Delhi pattern.
3. Cartoon from the Ramaynah. Subject: The Destruction of Lanka by Hanuman, the Monkey demi-god.

CONTENTS OF CASE I IN THE CENTRE OF COURT I.—
Mythological figures. The Hindu Pantheon.

1. Brahma.
2. Vishnu.   } These form the Hindu Trinity.
3. Shiva or Mahadeo.

4. Saraswati, goddess of learning, speech, &c., wife and daughter of Brahma.
5 to 14. The ten great incarnations of Vishnu.
5 to 31. All the usually recognised incarnations or Avatars of Vishnu.
5. The *Matsya* or Fish.
6. Kachh or Tortoise.
7. Varaha or Boar.
8. Nrisinha or Man Lion.
9. Vamana or Dwarf.
10. Parashu Rama, or Rama with the axe.
11. Rama Chandra or Rama, King of Ajudhya or Oude.
12. Krishn or Krishna.
13. Budh.

NOTE.—The arrangement is that adopted at Jeypore when the screens were temporarily erected, but the Royal Commission may have found it necessary to alter it in London.

14. Kalki. This incarnation is yet to come.

15. Vyasa, the author of the Puranas and arranger of the Vedas or Scriptures.

16. Rajah Pritha, first anointed king of earth.

17. Hari, Vishnu incarnate to release an elephant who called on his name.

18. Hansa, the goose or crane who taught the Vedas to Brahma.

19. Manu or Swayambhava, the first of the 14 Manus or great progenitors of mankind.

20. Yag or Yajna, sacrifice personified.

21. Rishabha, founder of the Jain religion, King of Oude.

22. Haya-Griva, the horse necked, who appeared to recover the Veda.

23. Dhruva, the polestar, a worshipper of Vishnu, who became incarnate in him, and was elevated to the polestar.

24. Dhanwantari, Physician of the Gods.

25. Badarinath, Vishnu as Lord of Badarinath in the Himalayas.

26. Dattatreya, a sage in whom a portion of the Trinity became incarnate.

27. Kapila, the sage, who destroyed the 160,000 sons of Sagara.

28 to 31. Sanaka, Sananda, Sanatana, Sanat-kumara. The four ever pure mind-born sons of Brahma or Vishnu.

32. $\left\{ \begin{array}{c} \text{Lakshmi} \\ \text{or} \\ \text{Sri} \end{array} \right\}$ wife of Vishnu, goddess of Fortune.

33. Ganga, or the river Ganges personified.

34 to 41. The regents of the nine planets.

34. Surya or the Sun, regent of the S. W. quarter.

35. Chandra, Soma, or the Moon, Regent of the N. E. quarter.

36. Mangala, the planet Mars.

37. Budha, the planet Mercury.

38. Brihaspati, the planet Jupiter.

39. Sukra, the planet Venus.

40. Sani, the planet Saturn.

41. Rahu, the ascending node personified as a dragon. The devourer of the sun and moon at eclipses.

42. Ketu, the descending node or lower part of Rahu.

43. Krishna holding up mount Govardhan to protect the cowherds against the wrath of Indra (Goranthan Nath.)

44. Bala Rama, elder brother of Krishna, an incarnation of the serpent Sesha.

45. Nagnathta hua Krishna, or Kali mantan. Krishna as destroyer of the Serpent King Kaliya, who lived in the Jamuna river.
46. Chatur-bhuja, the four-armed Vishnu.
47. Vishnu.
48. Sita, or Thakurani, wife of Rama Chandra.
49. Rukmini, wife of Krishna.
50. Hanuman, a demi-god, son of the wind and a monkey. The great general of Rama.
51. Narada, the sage, the friend of Krishna.
52. Garuda, the king of birds, the Vehicle of Vishnu.
53. Ganesh, Ganapati, the elephant-headed god of wisdom, invoked at the beginning of all work.
54. Parvati, wife of Siva.
55. Karttikeya, God of War, son of Siva.
56. Annaparna Devi, the bestower of food.
57. Sinha Vahani Devi, the great goddess Devi as conqueror of Rakhtavija, the demon.
58. Mahakali, or Devi as Durga, the destroyer of the demons, or All-devouring Time.
59. Mahisha-mardini Devi, the slayer of the demon Mahisha.
60. Kama, god of love, the Hindu Cupid-husband of Rati or Venus.
61. Indra, Regent of the Eastern Quarter, King of Heaven.
62. Indra, king of the gods as represented by the Jains.
63. Agni, Regent of the South-east, God of Fire.
64. Yama, Regent of the South, God of the Dead.
65. Varuna, Regent of the West, God of Water.
66. Vayu, Regent of the North-west, God of the Wind.
67. Vayu as father of Hanuman.
68. Kuvera, God of Wealth and Regent of the North, riding on a chariot.
69. Kuvera riding on a white horse.
70. Yamuna, the river Jumna personified.
71. Sila Deva, the form of the goddess Devi worshipped at Amber, the old capital of Jeypore.
72. Ananta, the king of Serpents on whom Vishnu reposes, Sesha-naga.
73. Mirritu, God of Death.
74 to 80. The seven forms of Krishna. If a worshipper looks at all the seven he can form some idea of the perfect Krishna.
74. Gokulish, Lord of Gokal. The image is now at Kamba and was formerly at Jeypore.

75. Madan Mohan, or Lord of Desire. Image now at Kamha, formerly at Jeypore.
76. Mathurish, Lord of Mathra, Temple at Kotah.
77. Vitalnath, Pandurang, at Kotah.
78. Dwarkanath, Lord of Dwarka. Temple at Kankeraoli in Meywar.
79. Srinath at Nathdwara in Meywar. This is the greatest and is not counted in the seven.
80. Naunaedpriya, the beloved of Nanda, or the infant Krishna at Nathdwara. Kada Nath at Surat has been omitted.
81. Bhairava, an inferior form of Siva.
82. Balmakund, the infant Krishna, god of the Valabacharyas.
83. The bull Nandi, the vehicle of Siva.
84. Sesha, king of Serpents, or lord of the lower world, who supports Vishnu while sleeping on the ocean during the intervals of creation.
85. Vishwakarma, Architect of the Gods.
86. Barbhagwan, or Vishnu as an infant floating on a leaf of the Indian fig before the creation.

SENTRY BOX AT THE END OF SCREEN A.

Above. Parvati, the Mountain Nymph, wife of Siva.

Below. Thakurani, wife of Vishnu or Rama.

SENTRY BOX AT THE END OF SCREEN B.

Above. Ganga, the Ganges.

Centre. Thakurani, wife of Krishna.

Below. Bala Rama, brother of Krishna.

COURT II.—POTTERY COURT.

BACK WALL—

1. Two marble panels from the plinth of the Cenotaph of Maharajah Sawai Jey Singh, Founder of Jeypore.
2. Cartoon from the Razmanamah. Subject: The birth of Parikshit.
3. Felts from Malpura.

SCREENS B. AND C.—

The shelves are filled with specimens of Jeypore Pottery, with the exception of two in one of the niches in Screen B, on which several fine carvings in marble are shewn.

FRONT ARCHWAY—

The panel in front is filled with pierced plaster and glass mosaic, and the shelf with an image in marble of Garuda, the vehicle of Vishnu, and with two painted figures of an elephant and a boat.

SENTRY BOX AT THE END OF SCREEN B.—

Pottery.

SENTRY BOX AT THE END OF SCREEN C.—

Figure of a *chela* or State servant.

The case in this Court should contain the enamel and gold jewellery, with ivory carvings and garnets.

COURT III.—METAL COURT.

BACK WALL—

1. Twelve rare old paintings from the private library of H. H. the Maharajah of Jeypore.
2. A large Brass Tray, Delhi pattern.
3. Cartoon from the Razmnamah. Subject : The Aswamedha, or the Great Horse Sacrifice.

SCREEN C.—

Top panels. Glass Mosaic.

Niches. Brass Trays, Lacquered Panels and Arms.

SCREEN D.—

Top panels. Brass Trays.

Niches. Brass Trays, Lacquered Panels. Arms.

FRONT ARCHWAY.—

Panel. Brass vessels of old form arranged in niches.

Shelf. Two lacquered wooden figures of a Camel and an Elephant; marble images of Ganesha, the god of wisdom ; and Nandi, the vehicle of Siva.

SENTRY BOX D.—

Brass Vessel.

CASE—

Silver Plate and Jewellery. Loans of H. H. the Maharajah of Jeypore, and fine Brass work.

COURT IV.—ETHNOLOGICAL COURT.

BACK WALL—

1. Cartoon from the Razmnamah. Subject : The lower depths of Hell as shewn to Yudhishthira.
2. Cartoon from the Razmnamah. Subject : Great Feast at Hastinapur.

SCREEN D.—

Top panel. Plaques of floral designs in plaster, glass, and coloured foil on a stone base.

Niches. Lacquered Panels and Arms.

SCREEN E.—

Top panel. Plaques in fresco and distemper.

Niches. Lacquered Panels and Arms.

FRONT ARCHWAY—

Front Panel. Mirror, mosaic.

Shelf. Pottery.

SENTRY BOX E—

Brass and Pottery.

CAR—

Models of heads of men of different castes in proper turbans.

COURT V.—SCHOOL OF ART COURT.

BACK WALL—

1. Cartoon from the Razmnamah. Subject : Hell as shewn to king Yudhishthira.
2. Rugs and *Durries* from the Jeypore jail.

SCREEN F.—

Top Shelf. Pottery and brass work.

Niche I. Carvings in stone.

Niche II. Incised lacquer.

SCREEN G.—

Top Shelf. Pottery and lacquer.

Niches. Pottery.

FRONT ARCHWAY—

Front Panel. Pierced plaster and glass mosaic.

Shelf. Pottery.

SENTRY BOX F.—

Model in papier maché of a Naga or Military ascetic.

SENTRY BOX G.—
  Brass models and vessels.
CASE.—
  Metal work from the School of Art, Jeypore.

COURT VI.—LACQUER COURT.

BACK WALL—
  1. Carved door from Chirawa.
  2. Brass tray.
  3. Cartoon from the Razmnamah. Subject: Departure of the White Horse from Hastinapur.
SCREEN G.—
  Top Panel. Tiles,
  Nidhet. Lacquer and arms.
SCREEN H.—
  Pierced carving in Teak Wood.
SANTRY BOX G.—
  Brass models and vessels.
SANTRY BOX H.—
  Above. Stone image of Mahadeo, Siva, or Shiva.
  Below. Stone Image of Hanuman.
CASE.—
  Lacquered Toys, Lac Bracelets, Betel-nut Carving, &c.
FLOOR OF THE NAKAR-KHANA OR DRUMHOUSE—
  Papiermache figures of Musicians and of women who drop garlands over the necks of distinguished persons; Musical instruments; the banner of the Imperial Assemblage; the standard of Jeypore; Sunshade borne before chiefs; and the Mahi Maratib or symbols of exalted rank given by the Emperors of Delhi.
CENTRAL AVENUE OR THE PICTURE GALLERY—
  1. Models in papier mache of a Rajput and his wife and of a Banker and his wife.
  2. The models of state vehicles and of buildings described in Chapter X.
  The collections of textiles, of domestic and sacrificial instruments, of astronomical models, of lacquered panels from the Razmnamah, and in short of all articles not shewn in the Provincial Courts will, it is understood, be found in the Picture Gallery.

www.ingramcontent.com/pod-product-compliance
Lightning Source LLC
Chambersburg PA
CBHW021427090426
42742CB00009B/1289